Every Day with Jesus

with Jesus

JUL/AUG 2018

Guaranteed

'For if you do these things, you will never stumble'
2 Peter 1:10

Selwyn Hughes
Revised and updated by Mick Brooks

CWR, Waverley Abbey House, Waverley Lane, Farnham, Surrey GU9 8EP, UK **Tel: 01252 784700**
Email: mail@cwr.org.uk Registered Charity No. 294387. Registered Limited Company No. 1990308.

MIX
Paper from
responsible sources
FSC® C015900

A word of introduction...

There have been numerous times when, having heard some faith-building talk or sermon – or read of someone who has just evangelised (and saved!) an entire village of people – I am totally inspired to go and do likewise. Yet I am often prone to then suffer a sense of residual guilt that, by Monday lunchtime, I still haven't seen an angel, a miracle or led three people to faith. Please don't misunderstand – all of that would be amazing, and I do believe in the extraordinary and the miraculous. But I do think we sometimes overcomplicate the Christian life, adding layers to compensate for the feeling that we have so little to bring to God and offer His people.

This issue is all about God's maths. Christianity is not about self-effort and 'must do better' techniques. Selwyn helps us explore how, as we take what feels like small faltering steps and offer what we can, God then does the multiplication. In a worldly sense, considerable time, effort and resources are invested in making ourselves more successful, and the pursuit of happiness has in itself become quite stressful. But Scripture reminds us that unstressed success is rooted ultimately in good character – not techniques, formulas, or programmes. It might sound obvious, but people naturally like and want to be around people of good character. So my prayer is that the notes in these two months to come will help you grow as you add your offering and God multiplies.

Mick Brooks, Consulting Editor

Abounding in Him

FOR READING & MEDITATION – 2 PETER 1:1–8

*'For if you possess these qualities in increasing measure,
they will keep you from being ineffective' (v8)*

In this issue we shall be focusing on three amazing verses found in the second letter of Peter (1:5–7), in which the apostle urges us to equip ourselves with a series of seven character qualities. This opening chapter of Peter's second letter gives us the impression that he was interested in mathematics, because he includes two spiritual sums. In verse 2 he says, 'Grace and peace be multiplied to you' (NKJV), and in verse 5, 'add to your faith, goodness… knowledge'. One is a multiplication sum, the other a sum of addition. God multiplies; we add. But it must be said that the adding only occurs as we grow in the grace that God multiplies to us.

In verses 3 and 4, Peter gives us a wonderful picture of the all-sufficiency of Jesus. In Him, we are told, there is endless power, overflowing generosity, great and precious promises. What is more, by virtue of our relationship with Him and through 'his very great and precious promises', we participate in the divine nature. However Peter concludes that it is possible to be beneficiaries of the divine nature and yet be 'ineffective and unproductive' (v8). In other words, it's possible to be rooted in Christ but not built up in Him. To be 'rooted' is to be in touch with divine resources; being 'built up' involves our co-operation. Jesus enables us to be participators in the divine nature; our part is to direct our energies into developing these seven great characteristics Peter identifies for us. And these seven qualities are not just in us, but are to be found in 'increasing measure'. In other words, they can overflow.

In Jesus there is not only life, but life abundant. We don't just exist in Him; we can flourish in Him.

FURTHER STUDY

John 15:1–17; Col. 2:1–7

1. How can we abound in Christ?

2. How do we abide in Christ?

God, forgive me if I am empty in the midst of plenty, ignorant in the midst of knowledge, lifeless in the midst of life. I place my empty cup into the stream of Your constant supply. Fill me to overflowing. In Jesus' name. Amen.

Never stationary

FOR READING & MEDITATION – 2 PETER 1:8–11

'For if you do these things, you will never fall' (v10)

Peter tells us that if we possess the seven qualities he identifies for us in verses 5 to 7 – goodness, knowledge, self-control, perseverance, godliness, brotherly kindness, and love – then 'we will never stumble or fall' (Amplified). Never? Surely he means that if we have these qualities we are not likely to stumble or fall? No, the apostle's statement is categorical. 'Do these things', he says, 'and you will never stumble or fall.' That is the guarantee we are given.

The first time I read those words I thought: *this takes some swallowing. How can one go through the Christian life without stumbling?* It depends, of course, on what we mean by 'stumbling'. I do not think Peter is saying that if we possess these seven qualities we will never again fall into sin. In my opinion, he is thinking of the Christian life in terms of a journey. When we add to our basic faith the seven characteristics he identifies, then we will never fall out of step, never get left behind; we will keep going until the journey's end.

FURTHER STUDY

1 John 2:1–29

1. What stages of Christian maturity does John identify?

2. How can we avoid walking in darkness and stumbling?

Without these qualities Peter tells us that we become 'short-sighted and blind' (v9). 'Short-sighted' because we see things only as they appear at the moment; 'blind' because we can't even see to take the next step. He tells us also that the Christian who does not realise the importance of adding to their faith this series of qualities will easily forget they have been cleansed from sin. As we remember daily, with gratitude, all that God has done for us in clearing the debt of sin that was against us, it enables and strengthens us on the journey (see Rom. 12:1–2). The Christian life is never stationary.

Father, help me I pray not to be a someone whose Christian life can be described as 'an initial enthusiasm followed by a chronic inertia'. I long to move ever onwards and upwards. Grant it may be so. In Jesus' name. Amen.

Do your best

FOR READING & MEDITATION – PHILIPPIANS 2:12–30

*'continue to work out your salvation with fear and trembling,
for it is God who works in you' (vv12–13)*

Yesterday we ended with the prayer that we would not be those whose Christian life could be described as 'an initial enthusiasm followed by a chronic inertia'. Many people might have a rush of excitement when they first realise the wonder of the Christian message, but then struggle to work out their salvation and make continuous progress.

Before looking in detail at the seven characteristics which we are to add to our basic faith in Christ, we first pause for a day or two to consider the words, 'Make every effort to add to your faith goodness, knowledge…' and so on (2 Pet. 1:5). Many Christians struggle to readily accept the instruction, 'Make every effort…' because it sounds like salvation by works. Yet, as we see from today's reading, the apostle Paul said something very similar. It is true that the Christian life is a life of faith and not works, but it is also true that a faith that does not lead to works might be no faith at all.

FURTHER STUDY

1 Cor. 15:58;
Eph. 2:8–10;
Heb. 4:1–11;
James 2:14–26

1. What is the place of faith and works?

2. What is the place of grace and effort?

The Christian community seems to go through phases of emphasis on this issue. It focuses on faith, with much less of an emphasis on the need to apply the principles of Scripture in our daily walk with Jesus, and then vice versa. This could be partly due to people's general lack of Bible engagement. John Stott once said, 'The low level of Christian living stems directly from the low level of Christian preaching.' One consequence of this lack of understanding is that, for many, there is a disconnect between belief and behaviour. When we live outside of God's instructions and guidelines as laid down in the Scriptures, we then face the consequences of not living the way God originally designed us to live.

Gracious and loving Father, I see even more clearly that faith without works is dead. Help me be someone whose faith shows itself in good and godly behaviour. This I ask in Jesus' name. Amen.

Just stretch!

FOR READING & MEDITATION – COLOSSIANS 3:1–17

'Put to death, therefore, whatever belongs to your earthly nature' (v5)

Before we finish considering the instruction, 'Make every effort...' let us be quite clear that we are not talking about willpower alone. Whenever human effort is emphasised, many are prone to regard it as an attempt to define living the Christian life simply by exercising our willpower, and label it 'legalism'. In *Your God is Too Safe*, Mark Buchanan says: 'We are overly prone to see legalism lurking behind every exhortation to strive and make an effort to be holy. Every time I say 'work out' your salvation, someone will hear me say 'work for' your salvation. The two are utterly different things.'

FURTHER STUDY

Josh. 14:6–14;
1 Chron. 4:10;
Psa. 18:21–36;
Isa. 54:1–3

1. How is our spiritual territory enlarged?

2. What did Caleb and Jabez share?

Many Christians do not fully understand the difference between grace and effort. They think that because they are saved by grace, they don't need to make an effort. Grace and effort are not opposites; grace and *earning* are opposites. The belief that you must work for your salvation is heretical; however, working out your salvation is biblical. 'Making every effort' involves the will, of course, but the effort we make to add to our faith the qualities that Peter outlines is not merely an exercise in willpower. There is a power working with our wills – the power of divine grace. As I have said so many times before, God supplies the power and we supply the willingness.

One commentator says that 'Make every effort' could be translated 'Just stretch!' He adds that, if we can't make the effort to stretch a little bit in the interests of our soul's development because we cannot be bothered by the inconvenience, then perhaps we don't have hold of the right thing. Do you believe you have got hold of the right thing? Good. Then stretch!

God, forgive me if I have let my spiritual life go and I'm out of condition. Please enable me to firm up my spiritual muscles. I know I have got hold of the right thing. Now help me to stretch. Amen.

CWR Ministry Events

PLEASE PRAY FOR THE TEAM

DATE	EVENT	PLACE	PRESENTER(S)
10 Jul	Inspiring Women Summer Evening	Waverley Abbey House	Marianne Needham-Bennett
11 Jul	Great Chapters of the Bible	WAH	Philip Greenslade
12–13 Jul	Leaders' Break	WAH	Andy Peck
28 Jul	Insight into Anxiety	WAH	Chris Ledger
20–24 Aug	Introduction to Biblical Care and Counselling	WAH	IBCC team
28 Aug	WAC Study Skills Day	WAH	Kathy Overton

Please pray for our students and tutors on our ongoing BA Counselling programme at Waverley Abbey College (which takes place at Waverley Abbey House), as well as our Certificate in Christian Counselling and MA Counselling qualifications.

We would also appreciate prayer for our ongoing ministry in Singapore and Cambodia, as well as the many regional events that will be happening around the UK this year.

For further information and a full list of CWR's courses, seminars and events, call **(+44) 01252 784719** or visit **www.cwr.org.uk/courses**

You can also download our free Prayer Track, which includes daily prayers, from **www.cwr.org.uk/prayertrack**

Faith is...

FOR READING & MEDITATION – JOHN 1:1–14

*'Yet to all who received him, to those who believed in his name,
he gave the right to become children of God' (v12)*

Now we begin to focus on the list of qualities that Peter tells us we must make every effort to add to our Christian lives (2 Pet. 1:5–7). Please notice, however, that the first thing he mentions – faith – is not something we have to add if we are Christians, but something we already possess. If faith is not there, then all attempts to add the qualities Peter lists amount to nothing more than moralism – religion reduced to moral practice. Spiritual growth may depend on adding one quality to another, but the Christian life begins in an act of faith. To put it another way: no one can become a Christian unless faith has been exercised.

FURTHER STUDY

Matt. 10:40;
Col. 1:1–14;
James 2:19;
1 John 5:1–13

1. Contrast merely holding a belief and faith.

2. How do we put our trust in God?

But what is faith? My favourite definition of faith is this: faith is welcoming that which you believe in. I like that definition because it emphasises that faith is more than mental belief; faith welcomes as a fact that which is believed as an idea. Today's text highlights that faith is not only believing but receiving. No definition of faith can be satisfactory if it confines faith merely to belief. That would make it the mental acknowledgment of some external fact and would not include the idea of trust.

Essentially, the key thought underlying the Greek word for faith (*pistis*) is that of trust. Faith, in the biblical sense, is not merely the holding of a belief; it is the venture of the whole personality in trusting one who is worthy to be trusted. The real end of biblical faith is to unite the person who believes with the person in whom one believes. Only as you are united with Christ in faith can you have the quality of life which is the foretaste of eternity.

Father, how can I ever sufficiently thank You for enabling me not only to believe in You but to receive Your Son into my heart and life? For that I shall be grateful for all eternity. Amen.

Launching out

FOR READING & MEDITATION – EPHESIANS 2:1–10

*'For it is by grace you have been saved, through faith
– and this not from yourselves, it is the gift of God' (v8)*

We will dwell for a few days on this matter of faith, in order to understand it a little more before we set about the task of making 'every effort' to add to it. The verse before us today – one of the great texts of Scripture – makes it clear that faith's ultimate source is God Himself: we are saved by grace, through faith, which is the gift of God. In some mysterious way, God comes to a person who is reaching out to Him and enables him or her to believe and receive. Notice the phrase 'believe and receive'. Believing that does not translate into receiving is not faith in the biblical sense of the word.

In the New Testament, faith is described in various ways – and each description contributes to a deeper understanding of the issue. In the Gospels, it is commonly connected with Jesus' healing miracles. Jesus was quick to detect faith, and His healing touch rested on those who, by faith, came to Him expecting a miracle. In the letters of Paul, faith is described as personal trust. He makes it clear that giving ourselves to Jesus opens the door through which we pass to turn our lives around. The letter to the Hebrews unfolds the fact that faith is a form of insight; it is the power to see reality behind appearance. For the apostle Peter, faith is the conviction that what Jesus Christ says is true and that we can rely on His Word and launch out on His promises (2 Pet. 1:4).

Faith, like swimming, is always an invitation to launch out and, like swimming also, we can never be sure until we do so. The mother who said that her little boy was not to go swimming until he knew how to swim had either to change her mind, or deny him the experience forever.

FURTHER STUDY

Num. 13:16–14:11;
Heb. 11:1–6

1. How can a lack of faith limit our experience of God?

2. How would you define faith in your own words?

My Father and my God, help me understand more of the faith that You have given me, not only so that I might know more about it but that I might venture more upon it. In Jesus' name I pray. Amen.

'A patron saint'

FOR READING & MEDITATION – JOHN 20:24–31

'Stop doubting and believe.' (v27)

Thomas has been called the 'Patron Saint of Doubt'. In many ways, it's a little sad that Thomas's one brief period of doubt has been remembered and spoken about to the extent that it eclipses everything else that we are told about him. We forget that he moved quickly beyond his doubts and was the first of the disciples (in Scripture at least) to confess that Jesus is God.

In any discussion on faith, it is necessary to understand the difference between unbelief and doubt – many Christians have been unnecessarily hindered by thinking their doubts to be unbelief. Simply, unbelief results from a closed mind, a mind that is firmly set against believing. Doubt is different, however; doubt says, 'I am not sure about this, but if it is true then I want to believe it.'

One of the things that has surprised me in my life is how doubts can mingle so freely with faith. There are times when I find myself caught up intimately with God in prayer and yet a doubt buzzes around for a few moments, like a fly against a window pane, and suggests, 'Aren't you really talking to yourself?' However, although doubt may visit those in whose heart faith in God exists, we need not allow it to make a home within our mind.

The universe in which we live was made and is held together by God's Son (Heb. 1:2). Equally, our lives are held in God's hands, who is always seeking to enter into human life but is often frustrated by unbelief. We read that Jesus was unable to do many miracles in Nazareth because of the people's unbelief (Matt. 13:58). Faith provides a point of entry for God's power to come through. When people believe utterly, it comes through as a flood.

FURTHER STUDY

Matt. 13:53–58;
17:14–21;
Mark 9:14–27

1. How do these accounts show that doubt and belief can co-exist?

2. How can belief overcome doubt?

Father, thank You for reminding me once again of the difference between doubt and unbelief. Help me more and more to doubt my doubts and believe my beliefs. In Jesus' name I pray. Amen.

What faith feeds on

FOR READING & MEDITATION – ROMANS 10:14–21

'faith comes from hearing the message, and the message is heard through the word of Christ.' (v17)

I believe it was C.S. Lewis who observed that if you took a hundred people who had turned away from the Christian faith, you would find that very few of them had been argued out of it. Rather, you would discover that they had drifted away because they did not feed their faith on the Word of God.

We live dangerously when we neglect the Bible. As today's text reminds us, 'faith comes from hearing the message, and the message is heard through the word of Christ.' When we read God's Word, we are listening to His voice, and faith grows under the sound of that voice. Mature Christians know that time spent studying the Bible feeds their faith more than anything else. God has scattered through the Scriptures what Peter calls 'very great and precious promises' (2 Pet. 1:4), and faith grows by engaging with those promises and believing them.

I wonder if anyone remembers the 'promise boxes' that used to be found in the homes of some Christians. These boxes contained rolled up pieces of paper, on which were printed promises found in the Bible. When you visited a home, you were invited to select a promise from the promise box, usually just before you left. This practice eventually came in for a lot of criticism, mainly because people quite rightly argued that the Bible contains much more than promises, but also because there are times when what is really needed is not so much a word to comfort the challenged as a word to challenge the comfortable. Yet even though 'promise boxes' were sometimes misused, the preoccupation with God's promises was far healthier than the attitude of many of today's Christians who give no time to searching out God's promises to lay hold of them.

FURTHER STUDY

Josh. 1:1–9;
Psa. 1:1–6;
119:161–168

1. How would Joshua have courage and success?

2. What assurances do we find in the psalms?

Father, help me take to heart the truth I have learned today that the more time I spend studying Your Word, the more my faith will grow. I love Your Word; please help me love it even more. In Jesus' name. Amen.

Faith – an act

FOR READING & MEDITATION – LUKE 17:11–19

*'When he saw them, he said, "Go, show yourselves to the priests."
And as they went, they were cleansed.' (v14)*

Yesterday we saw that faith grows by exposing our minds to the truths contained in God's Word, and engaging with His promises. Another way faith grows is by acting upon it. This is how one writer helps us understand faith: 'Picture a fledgling eaglet peering over the nest into the empty air. Is it possible that the air can hold it up? Is it not plain madness to push out into space? Does not death await the little bird if it ventures out of the nest? But some instinct stirs within its little breast and it spreads its wings. Or the mother destroys the nest and snatches its security away. Over the edge it goes and proves that the empty air is the element devised in order to hold it, and not only to hold it, but lift it to the upper skies.' How we need to spread our wings and allow the great winds of the Holy Spirit to bear us aloft. God can do great things where there is faith.

I had already completed the next section when the Spirit whispered that what I had written was not what He wanted me to say. So here is the message He gave me: Do you need a miracle in your life today – something you know it is right to ask God for? Then have faith for it.

Not long after I became a Christian, my father wrote these words in my Bible: 'Faith is an affirmation and an act that bids eternal truth be fact.' We *act* faith as well as affirm it. The ten lepers in the passage before us acted on Jesus' instructions. We read, 'As they went, they were cleansed.' In the act of obedience, faith turned to fact and healing followed. It's important to test if it's God's voice you hear, by checking with others and His Word. But if it is, don't hesitate – do it.

FURTHER STUDY

Isa. 40:28–31;
Matt. 14:22–33;
John 9:1–7

1. Is your faith an attitude or an action?

2. How can we experience miracles?

Father, I realise that faith is not just an affirmation but also an act. Forgive me that so often I wait for You to act when You are waiting for me to act. I believe. Now help me act on my belief. In Jesus' name. Amen.

'A sound of double bolting'

FOR READING & MEDITATION – PSALM 77:1–20

'Has God forgotten to be merciful? Has he in anger withheld his compassion?' (v9)

Faith also has the opportunity to grow in situations of ambiguity and uncertainty. Anyone can have faith when the sun is shining and there are no dark clouds in the sky, but what happens when storms come and we are pounded by the winds of hardship and adversity? Well, what we should not do is pretend that we are not stunned by them. If we are not stunned by them then fine, but if we are then we admit that we are. There is no shame in this. God will not fall off His throne because your faith has been rocked. We are not all like Abraham who 'staggered not at the promise of God' (Rom. 4:20, KJV) when he was told by God that his wife Sarah was to have a child at the grand old age of 90.

When C.S. Lewis' wife Joy died of cancer, this is what he wrote about the spiritual fog in which he found himself: 'Go to [God] when your need is desperate, when all other help is in vain, and what do you find? A door slammed in your face, and a sound of bolting and double bolting on the inside. After that, silence. You might as well turn away.' One writer said that Lewis' words at that time were blasphemous. No, he wasn't being blasphemous, he was being real. Lewis did not turn away. In fact, he came through the experience with God's help, and readers of Lewis' works came to hear a new note in his writings. The story of how he found God in the midst of his pain has become a classic account of how faith can not only survive but thrive in times of despair.

Are there some dark clouds in your life at the moment? Hold on. When you come through the time of difficulty, you will find that there are more muscles in your faith than you could ever have thought possible.

FURTHER STUDY

1 Kings 19:1–19;
Job 1:13–2:10;
42:1–10

1. How did Elijah come through his crisis?

2. What was Job's experience?

Father, help me in times of discouragement to be real enough not only to admit what I am feeling, but also to recognise that You are there even though my feelings are not registering the fact. In Jesus' name. Amen.

Faith at its best

FOR READING & MEDITATION – 2 KINGS 6:8–23

'And Elisha prayed, "O LORD, open his eyes so that he may see."
Then the LORD opened the servant's eyes' (v17)

Before leaving this issue of faith, let me paint a picture of someone in whom faith is growing. He or she will not claim that their faith never staggers or that there is an absence of doubt, but they will become increasingly confident that God knows best in all things. A growing faith comes to see that this is God's world and believes it, as W.E. Sangster said, 'not by shutting one's eyes to the apparent contradictions that are in the world but by believing that to God there are none'. Faith is always at its best and is most robust when it has faith in the faithfulness of God. When we can see that the apparent contradictions only disguise the love which burns in all things, then we are really growing.

FURTHER STUDY

Dan. 3:1–30;
Heb. 11:7–40

1. How did the three Hebrews express their faith?

2. How do we see the invisible God?

After nearly 60 years as a Christian, I cannot claim to be where I would like to be in this matter of faith, but I am much further on than I was. Perhaps you may share my feeling. Elisha prayed for his servant in the story we have read today. The king of Syria had flung a wide circle of horses and chariots around the city, and when the prophet's servant awoke the next morning and saw the city besieged, he was extremely disturbed. But Elisha himself was unperturbed. However, to calm the fears of his servant, 'Elisha prayed, "O LORD, open his eyes so that he may see." Then the LORD opened the servant's eyes, and he looked and saw the hills full of horses and chariots of fire'. In the words of one poet, 'Lo, to faith's enlightened sight, all the mountains flame with light.'

I have often stopped and prayed for readers of these notes and asked that their faith might go on growing and like Elisha's servant their eyes will be opened also.

Gracious and loving Father, enlighten our faith until we see, and see clearly, that 'all the mountains flame with light'. In Jesus' name. Amen.

A supporting cast

FOR READING & MEDITATION – EPHESIANS 5:1–14

*'For you were once darkness, but now you are light in the Lord.
Live as children of light' (v8)*

Soon after I became a Christian in my teens, my pastor drew my attention to 2 Peter 1:5 and said: 'These are the qualities that God now wants you to add to your faith. Faith has to have a "supporting cast" in order to be effective.' Then, changing the metaphor, he continued: 'But don't try to get them all at once. Make sure your feet are on the first rung of the ladder before you attempt the second.' That was good advice and something that I, in turn, have passed on to many new to faith.

The first thing that has to be added to faith, says Peter in 2 Peter 1:5, is goodness. The Greek word translated 'goodness' (*arete*) is rarely used in the New Testament and, according to Greek scholars, is best understood as 'excellence'. Eugene Peterson's *The Message* reads 'good character', and most likely that is what Peter had in mind when he used the word *arete*. This begs the question: Is this good character of which Peter speaks something that comes as a result of willpower, or is it something that God deposits within us? Well, it is both.

The day after I invited Jesus Christ into my life, I went out into my old surroundings amid the old temptations and found to my astonishment that many of them had lost their hold on me. I simply didn't want them. I didn't need them. I realised that there was a new strength in my life, which was the sign of His presence. But I knew instinctively that this new inner strength would not develop without my co-operation. I could not lie back and say, 'I am now invulnerable to temptation.' I still had to make the decision daily to give my life to Jesus, and put off my old sinful habits such as telling lies. God's power and my willingness had to combine.

FURTHER STUDY

1 Pet. 2:1–12;
1 Thess. 5:1–11

1. Why does faith need a 'supporting cast'?

2. How are we to encourage one another?

Father, I am so grateful for the truth that as I hold on to You, You hold on to me. This is so wonderful. May I always be willing to work with You, Lord. Amen.

Beauty from brokenness

Patrick Regan, author of *When Faith Gets Shaken* and *Honesty Over Silence*, and founder of XLP, talks to CWR about Kintsugi Hope – the charity that he and his wife Diane have recently founded – and how they are working to bring light and treasure to dark and broken places...

Patrick – what is Kintsugi Hope?

Following a series of operations, illnesses and losses that took us to the brink physically, mentally, emotionally and spiritually, we produced *When Faith Gets Shaken* to talk about our experiences. In opening up about our struggles, we realised how many people have felt alone in theirs – and the great need for each of us to be vulnerable, open and honest when life is hard. Only when this happens can healing start to take place.

We wanted to take this a step further by creating safe and supportive spaces for people suffering with mental and emotional health issues – and so Kintsugi Hope was born. 'Kintsugi' (which means 'golden joinery') is the Japanese technique for repairing pottery with seams of gold. This repairs the brokenness in a way that makes the object more beautiful than it was prior to being broken. Instead of hiding the scars, it makes a feature of them.

What kinds of issues will you be addressing?

Over recent years, much has been done to raise awareness about emotional and mental health challenges – but we need to do more not only to raise awareness but to offer people support who are going through these challenges. We will be writing and running a course on mental and emotional wellbeing, which we hope to deliver in coffee shops, schools, prisons, churches and in homes – anywhere people come together. We will also produce resources on issues such as anger, perfectionism, shame, anxiety and depression.

Internationally, we are hoping to work with people whose mental health has been affected by war, trauma and poverty, particularly within the refugee community, and advocate for them in Westminster.

How will you be partnering with CWR?

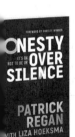

We've written a book called *Honesty Over Silence*, which seeks to open up conversations around topics that many find difficult (such as dealing with anxiety and depression, the challenges of parenting a child with special needs, among other things), and looks at how we can live authentically and honestly as we grow into the people God created us to be.

We are so excited that Kintsugi Hope is going to be partnering with CWR as there is so much synergy between the two organisations. We both want to communicate God's love in a way that sees transformation of the whole person.

For more information, visit **www.kintsugihope.com**

Honesty Over Silence is available from July.
ISBN: 978-1-78259-833-6
For price and to purchase, visit **www.cwr.org.uk/shop**
or use the order form at the back of these notes.

Like a child

FOR READING & MEDITATION – MATTHEW 18:1–9

'Therefore, whoever humbles himself like this child is the greatest in the kingdom of heaven.' (v4)

Goodness, which we said yesterday is best understood as good or excellent character, when divorced from the Holy Spirit's power, degenerates into the thing we mentioned earlier – moralism. Those who are purely moralistic tend to have a superior air and look down on those who struggle with moral issues.

One of the marks of a Christian who draws on God's strength in living out the Christian life is humility. Jesus taught that humility is the pre-eminent characteristic of those who belong to His kingdom (Matt. 5:3). In today's passage, He speaks of the need to have humility like that of a child. Many people find this statement difficult to understand since, as one commentator says, 'Children are seldom humble in either character or conduct.' So what did Jesus mean when He made this puzzling statement? What He had in mind, I think, was the idea of status rather than behaviour. Children, as you know, are often referred to as 'dependants' – they depend on their parents for everything. The humility of a child, then, is the humility of dependence. Few things are as off-putting as arrogance, and that is what you might find in moralism. On the other hand, nothing is more endearing than humility, and that is what you find in those who depend on God for the strength to live a good and moral life.

If Jesus needed to live in dependence on His Father, then how can we do less than ask God for the strength to live our lives in the right way? And He gives that strength to us through the blessed Holy Spirit.

FURTHER STUDY

Micah 6:8;
Luke 7:36–50;
18:9–17

1. What does God require of us?

2. What different things did the Pharisees and sinners depend on?

Heavenly Father, I am Your child, one of Your 'dependants'. Help me understand the implications of this fact and to walk before You with the humility that comes from knowing this deep truth. In Jesus' name. Amen.

When the mind functions best

FOR READING & MEDITATION – 1 JOHN 5:6–12

'For there are three that testify: the Spirit, the water and the blood'
(vv7–8)

One of the things I have found both as a pastor and a counsellor is that moral problems are often concealed behind intellectual problems. We can develop a problem in our minds in order to divert attention away from what is going on in our soul.

A man once came to me with questions about the Trinity. He told me he was troubled by intellectual doubts concerning this great doctrine of the Christian faith. So I said, 'The teaching concerning the Trinity is difficult to understand and we cannot comprehend it unless we are given spiritual insight; the truth is more "overheard" in the Bible and we come to it by revelation.' I then used an illustration from the works of Saint Augustine, who wrote, 'Go to the Jordan and you will see the Trinity.' There at Jesus' baptism, the three Persons in the Godhead are simultaneously in evidence. The Father speaks directly from heaven, the Son is immersed in the river, and John the Baptist sees the Spirit descending upon the Son. However, it was clear that much of what I was saying was being lost on this man. But by a swift insight given, I believe, by the Holy Spirit, I saw into his soul. I put my hand on his and asked, 'Are you struggling with a moral problem?' His eyes dropped. He confessed that he was, and we left the doctrine of the Trinity to deal with the problem in his soul. After prayer and counselling, I am glad to say this problem was resolved.

What happened, though, with his intellectual problems concerning the Trinity? Some time later, he told me, 'I still don't understand the doctrine, but for some reason I am no longer uncomfortable with it.' The mind functions best when the soul is right before God.

FURTHER STUDY

Psa. 51:1–19; John 4:7–29

1. How might the religious debate exclude God?

2. How did Jesus conclude the debate?

My Father and my God, save me from developing a problem in my mind to hide a problem in my soul. You desire truth in the inner parts. May I be the kind of person You want me to be. In Jesus' name. Amen.

Soul surgery

FOR READING & MEDITATION – 2 CORINTHIANS 13:1–10

'Examine yourselves to see whether you are in the faith; test yourselves.' (v5)

The moral maze, as we saw yesterday, can often contribute to intellectual blindness. In a moral world the most critical thing is moral response, and therefore, as Christians, we need to check ourselves regularly to make sure that our lives do not fall short when it comes to moral matters.

In his book *Strengthening Your Grip*, Charles Swindoll tells of a doctor in New York, Dr Evan O'Neill, who was so convinced that some major operations could be performed while the patients were under a local anaesthetic that, to prove his point, he operated on himself and removed his appendix under local anaesthetic. The operation was a success, and he recovered much faster than is usual after such a procedure.

FURTHER STUDY

Exod. 20:16;
Psa. 139:23–24;
Matt. 5:8;
Eph. 4:17–32

1. How can we check our spiritual health?

2. Why should we check it?

May I suggest that you consider 'operating' on yourself as we go through these studies together? Not physically, of course, but spiritually. We could call this 'self-exploratory surgery of the soul'. Fully conscious and fully aware, allow the Holy Spirit to assist you as He hands you the only instrument you need – the virus-free scalpel of Scripture.

Begin by considering this question: Can I be depended upon to tell the truth in all situations? After becoming a Christian, I found it hard to stop telling lies. But I knew that Jesus never lied, nor does He give us a licence to lie. As mentioned previously, I had a new inner strength to help me to stop telling lies – but at the same time I had to make a deliberate decision to stop lying. The Early Christians, standing before tribunals, could have saved their lives with a little lie, but they chose not to – and in many cases, the consequence was martyrdom.

Heavenly Father, give me the courage to speak the truth, the whole truth, and nothing but the truth – everywhere and always. In Jesus' name. Amen.

Beware of rationalisation

FOR READING & MEDITATION – MATTHEW 25:14–30

*'"Master," he said, "I knew that you are a hard man,
harvesting where you have not sown"' (v24)*

We continue considering the question: Can I be depended upon to tell the truth in all situations? What about being honest with ourselves? Have you heard these words from Shakespeare's *Hamlet* before?

> *This above all: to thine own self be true,*
> *And it must follow, as the night the day*
> *Thou can'st not then be false to any man.*

Many of us have within us the tendency to indulge in 'rationalisation'. In today's parable, the man given the one talent blamed his master for his failure and made excuses by saying he had been unable to make any gains because his master was a hard man. That was rationalisation.

Here is another example: a man allows himself to fall in love with another man's wife, and then proceeds to rationalise the whole affair by talking to himself about the sacredness of this feeling of love. Soon, black looks like white. He is self-deceived. As we know from the Bible, David did something very much like this with Bathsheba (see 2 Sam. 11:1–27).

Human consciousness has an amazing capacity for self-deception because it disowns or denies the ugly things that are within us. Can you answer this question with me now: Am I willing to root out of my life every dishonest thing, no matter how difficult a struggle it may be? Your decision may involve restitution. Even though it is not always possible to make restitution, are we willing to do so if we are able to? Make the decision never to rationalise. Doing so is incompatible with moral excellence.

FURTHER STUDY

Exod. 20:13–17;
2 Sam.
11:1–12:13

1. How could David have avoided sin?

2. How was David convicted of sin?

Father, may there be no infection in my soul, no open wounds. I long to be the person You want me to be. From now on, no rationalisation. In Jesus' name. Amen.

Pure desire

FOR READING & MEDITATION – MATTHEW 5:21–30

'I tell you that anyone who looks at a woman lustfully has already committed adultery with her in his heart.' (v28)

Without doubt, one of the biggest battles we have in order to grow in good character is around the matter of sex. Billy Graham suggested that there is no greater battle in life than the one around sex. So how do we prepare ourselves for this battle?

First, we acknowledge the fact that sexual desire is part of human nature. To act as though there is no such thing as sex is to repress the desire and drive it deeper into the subconscious. And that is fertile ground for emotional turmoil. Most people will experience sexual desire, some more than others. There is no shame in this. It is part of our makeup. The question is not so much whether we have sexual desire but whether it has us. As a servant, sex gives drive to the personality; as a master, it leads to devastation. A young Christian man once wrote to me and commented, 'I do go with other women, but I would not consider myself to be a philanderer.' How blind and how self-deceived.

FURTHER STUDY

Gen. 39:1–23;
Prov. 6:20–32

1. How did Joseph resist temptation?

2. Why may an uncontrolled sexual desire destroy us?

As Christians, we belong to the one who, as we can see from today's passage, set the place of responsibility not merely in the physical act but in the inward thought also. Let's continually ask God to help us keep our thought life pure. And don't be like St Augustine who, when he was struggling with sexual desire, is said to have prayed, 'Lord, make me pure, but not right now.' If you have not done so before, then surrender your sexuality to God now. A great historian wrote, 'The moral law is written into everything.' Those who obey the moral law get results; those who break it face the consequences. Make up your mind to be of good character in the area of sex, as in all other areas of life.

Father, take me by the hand so that I am not led by sexual desire. Help me to be pure and of good character. In Jesus' name. Amen.

'Unbinding inner cords'

FOR READING & MEDITATION – 1 JOHN 1:1–10

'If we confess our sins, he is faithful and just and will forgive us our sins' (v9)

We continue to reflect on the need to add to our faith this important quality of good character. If there is anything doubtful in our lives, anything that does not come up to the standards of God's Word, then we need to be rid of it.

An evangelist who travelled around the world once told me that he used to put his Bible on top of the clothes in his suitcase, so that customs inspectors would see that he was religious and not search for undeclared dutiable items which were at the bottom of the case. He also told me that whenever he preached, a little voice (the voice of conscience) said, 'You are not the man other people think you are.' When he decided to have done with such dishonesty, his ministry took on a new power.

If we have been the kind of people prepared to have a Bible plus hidden dutiable articles, then we need to move away from that way of life as quickly as possible. One preacher describes owning up to such behaviour as 'exteriorising our rottenness'. The editor of a newspaper in India told me that he had published false reports in his paper, but later confessed publicly that he had done so. He was heavily criticised for admitting to his guilt but he said, 'That confession unbound the inner cords that were tying up my soul.'

There is an old saying that 'confession is good for the soul'. It is. But to whom do we confess our wrongdoing? Confess it first to God. If others have been affected, confess it to them also. If others have not been affected, then the matter is one that should be dealt with between God and you alone. We do not need to broadcast our failures to everyone. God deals with some things in His private office.

FURTHER STUDY

Psa. 32:1–11; 38:1–22; Isa. 59:1–3

1. What happens when we hide our sin?

2. What happens when we confess our sin?

Dear God, in this matter of good character, dare I close my heart to You? I cannot. I will not. I come just as I am. Make me morally pure. Make me clean. In Jesus' name. Amen.

'Some things are closed... '

FOR READING & MEDITATION – PSALM 119:97–104

'I have more insight than all my teachers, for I meditate on your statutes.' (v99)

Once we have committed ourselves to being men and women of good character, the next thing we make every effort to add to our faith, says the apostle Peter, is knowledge (2 Pet. 1:5). But what kind of knowledge? Worldly knowledge? Academic knowledge? No. What Peter has in mind, I think, is spiritual knowledge – the knowledge that comes through intimacy with God and His Word. The Greek word translated 'knowledge' – *gnosis* – has to do with practical knowledge that enables a person to make the right decisions and apply the right principles.

FURTHER STUDY

Psa. 119:89–96,105–112,129–144

1. What are the benefits of studying God's Word?

2. Upon what did the psalmist set his heart?

William Barclay described it as the kind of knowledge 'that enables us to act honourably and efficiently in the day-to-day circumstances of life'. *The Message* translates this as 'spiritual understanding'.

A Christian counsellor once talked to me about an approach they used in their practice that was quite clearly unbiblical. When I pointed this out to the counsellor their response was, 'But it works.' 'Surely the issue is not whether it works,' I said, 'but whether it is right.' Pragmatism should not serve as a guide; the only reliable guide is the Bible, where God has laid down all the principles we need in order to live an effective life for Him. One person has suggested that if you treat the word 'Bible' as an acrostic, the letters could stand for 'Basic Instructions Before Leaving Earth'.

In today's text, the psalmist declared that meditating on God's Word had given him more insight than all his teachers. Scripture provided him with insight that enabled him to see beyond what is apparent in life and into the heart of things. Some matters in this universe are, sadly, closed to secular minds.

Father, help me grasp the fact that the unfolding of Your Word gives light – light that I cannot get from any other source. Help me to walk in that light with a sure and steady tread. In Jesus' name. Amen.

CWR Today

Pursuing fullness and freedom

*'The thief comes only to steal and kill and destroy; I have come that they may have **life**, and have it to the full.'* John 10:10

Mental health issues, and other often misunderstood challenges, prevent many people from living in fullness and freedom.

CWR's *Insight* series has been developed in response to the great need to help people understand and work through key issues that many of us struggle with today, such as anxiety, depression, stress, anger and self-acceptance.

The *Insight* books and courses take caring for your own mental health – and the health of others – beyond the therapeutic to Biblical application, with insight from experts in the field of mental health.

We need to break through the misconceptions around mental health issues, dismiss the damaging labels and make mental health a priority in our churches. And you can help us.

£25 could subsidise a regional *Insight* course for two people.

£45 enables the development of *Insight* books and courses for a younger audience.

£70 will assist with costs for filming and producing multimedia versions of our *Insight* series courses to reach a wider audience.

To donate, please use the order form at the back of these notes, or visit **www.cwr.org.uk/donate**

Thank you.

'Education without God...'

FOR READING & MEDITATION – COLOSSIANS 2:1–15

'My purpose is that they may... have the full riches of complete understanding' (v2)

The knowledge the apostle Peter talks about in 2 Peter 1:5 is not the knowledge that comes from studying any system of education devised by the world, but from an acquaintance with God and His Word. There is nothing wrong, of course, in gaining a good secular education, but we must differentiate between secular knowledge and spiritual knowledge. A person can be highly educated but be quite uninformed when it comes to the really important issues of life. Lloyd George, a former British prime minister, once famously said, 'Education without God makes clever devils.' Today we have some very 'clever devils' emerging from our colleges and universities.

FURTHER STUDY

1 Cor. 2:1–16;
Eph. 1:15–23;
3:1–21

1. How do we experience revelation?

2. What is the difference between mental and spiritual knowledge?

There is a general agreement among educators that basically there are three methods of 'knowing': intuition, rational thought, and empiricism. Sometimes we 'know' that a certain way to do something is right, even though we have no objective reason for our actions. That is intuition. Rational thought helps us come up with good reasons why we should do what we should do. Here logic and reason prevail. Empiricism, which involves experimentation, helps us 'know' things through trial and error.

Christians, however, have another source of knowledge – revelation. Without revelation (God's disclosure of Himself through the living Word and the written Word), we would never know how to become experts in the art of living. One university student allegedly tore up his degree certificate and sent it back to the university where he had been educated saying, 'You taught me how to make a living but you never taught me how to live.' Only God's Word teaches us how to live life well and to the full.

Father, how grateful I am for the truths contained in the pages of Your Word, the Bible. It enlightens my mind with the truth, redirects my will, cleanses my emotions, and sets me up to live abundantly. Amen.

The challenge of our times

FOR READING & MEDITATION – PSALM 119:25–32

'I have chosen the way of truth; I have set my heart on your laws.'
(v30)

We stay with the main issue discussed yesterday, that those who are searching for practical knowledge that enables them to make the right decisions and apply the right principles need to turn first to the Scriptures. The Bible is God's one and only published work, which is designed to help us become experts in the art of living.

However, let's face the fact that the age through which we are passing gives the Bible little attention and is quickly dismissed as irrelevant. It's forgotten that it is, by far, the world's bestselling book and upon its writings whole nations and cultures have, in times past, based their moral and legal and political systems. The time in which we live has been described as the era of postmodernism. This concept, which is prevalent in our colleges and universities, says that all claims to truth are relative to other claims, and therefore all ideas and truth must be treated as equal. This kind of thinking is influencing many young Christians, and that is why we need to ensure that we do not allow the world to squeeze us into its own mould. In my opinion, postmodernism is the greatest challenge to the gospel since the Enlightenment, which questioned tradition and authority and emphasised reason.

I remember as a young student having many questions about the reliability and authority of the Bible, but once I accepted it by faith as God's revelation and stopped trying to make it fit into my thinking, it became a new book to me. One of my spiritual mentors used to say: 'The Bible is not true because it satisfies reason, but it satisfies reason because it's true.' Accept it by faith and you too will find it will become a new book for you.

FURTHER STUDY

Psa. 119:33–56;
2 Pet. 1:19–21

1. Why is the Bible superior to any other book?

2. Why might people reject it?

God, help me in these challenging times, when Your eternal Word is being dismissed as irrelevant, to hold fast to its truths, principles and its precepts. Deepen my confidence in its reliability and sufficiency I pray. In Jesus' name. Amen.

A response to revelation

FOR READING & MEDITATION – HOSEA 4:1–9

'my people are destroyed from lack of knowledge.' (v6)

One thing is sure: those who reject the Bible's reliability will not get very far in the Christian life. John Stott wrote: 'I am not saying that it is impossible to be a disciple of Jesus without a high view of Scripture... yet I venture to add that a full, balanced and mature Christian discipleship is impossible whenever disciples do not submit to their Lord's teaching authority as it is mediated through Scripture.' I agree.

In fact, I would go further and say that those Christians who make every effort to add to their faith the qualities that Peter lists in the first chapter of his second epistle but do not accept the Bible as the final authority in all things spiritual, are pursuing a pointless task. Our Christian life is effective only when we respond to revelation and is seriously impaired if we do not depend on a reliable, objective revelation of God. This is a crucial issue and we must come down on one side or the other.

Those who operate by reason alone pour scorn on us when we say that we take the Bible by faith, because they argue that by doing so we suspend our reason. But reason is an inadequate guide. The eighteenth-century world saw the dawning of what was described as 'The Age of Reason'. But where has it led us? Mental health professionals dealing with pandemic anxiety and depression. While the unfolding of God's Word gives light, it is also true that the neglect of His Word brings darkness. The lifestyle we have developed results in shattered nerves, tangled lives and broken homes. We seem to know everything about life except how to live it. When we neglect the Bible and its truths, we do so at our peril.

FURTHER STUDY

Matt. 7:24–29;
John 20:30–31;
Acts 17:10–12;
1 Tim. 4:13

1. Why is the Bible so important?

2. Why do people reject it?

God my Father, save Your people from being squeezed into the mould of the many. May we become known once again as 'The People of the Book'. This I ask in Jesus' name. Amen.

Jesus' view of Scripture

FOR READING & MEDITATION – MARK 12:1–12

'Haven't you read this scripture: "The stone the builders rejected has become the capstone?"' (v10)

We are considering that the spiritual understanding that we are to add to the quality of goodness is that which is immersed in Scripture. We are saying also that the Bible is often quickly dismissed, and that our critics accuse us of committing intellectual suicide when we assert that we accept its truths.

One reason why Christians take this stance is because that was Jesus' attitude to Scripture. In every area of Christ's life – His ethical conduct, His public debates with the religious leaders, His teaching times with His disciples – His primary concern was always to be true to Scripture. He would frequently refer to the Scriptures and ask: 'But how then would the Scriptures be fulfilled?' (Matt. 26:54) or 'Haven't you read this scripture?' The Old Testament was always His final court of appeal.

The question may be raised: Jesus accepted the Old Testament but what about the New? Well, of course the New Testament was not written during Jesus' days on earth, but He made provision for it to be written by equipping His apostles to be the teachers of His Church, and He anticipated His followers would listen to them. 'He who listens to you listens to me', He said, and 'he who rejects you rejects me' (Luke 10:16). This implies that submission to the teaching of the apostles in Scripture is part of our submission to Jesus as Lord, for 'a student is not above his teacher' (Luke 6:40). We cannot claim to follow Jesus and dismiss His view of the Word of God. I know there are those who claim to be submitted to Christ, yet do not accept the authority of the Bible. But, to again quote John Stott, 'selective submission is not authentic submission'.

FURTHER STUDY

Matt. 4:1–11;
15:1–9;
Luke 4:14–27;
17:26–37

1. How did Jesus avoid sin?

2. How did Jesus use and rely on Scripture?

Heavenly Father, if there are any doubts in my heart regarding the truth and reliability of Scripture, then let the truth I have pondered today put them finally to rest. Your Son believed Your Word. So will I. Amen.

The purpose of Scripture

FOR READING & MEDITATION – 2 TIMOTHY 3:10–17

'All Scripture is God-breathed and is useful for teaching, rebuking, correcting and training in righteousness' (v16)

The Bible has many purposes, not least being a manual of instruction. It contains many deep truths that we need to ponder, but we do not reap the full benefits of the Bible unless we read it in order to learn how to apply its principles to everyday life and relationships.

In the text before us today, the emphasis is not just on knowing Scripture but on living it. Scripture, we are told, is useful – but useful for what? For learning about the geography of Israel and the surrounding nations? For knowing the customs of the Middle East? Well, maybe, but that is not what the apostle Paul has in mind. It is intended to shape us and help us to walk in righteousness and apply God's Word to every situation in life. If we are not engaging with the Word of God for that purpose, then we are misunderstanding it.

FURTHER STUDY

Psa. 119:1–24;
Isa. 55:8–9

1. How can we avoid sin?

2. Why is God's Word essential to daily living?

Do you know what to do if someone has something against you? You can find the information in Matthew 18. Do you know the principles that help bind a marriage? You'll find them in Ephesians 5. Do you want to know how to discipline your children? Then turn to Ephesians 6. Are you having difficulty relating to someone over you in authority? Look up Paul's instructions on this issue in Romans 13.

Those who regard the Bible only as a theological textbook written to give us insights into the nature of God are missing the point. Please don't misunderstand me; it *is* that, of course. But the Bible has also been given to us as a manual of instruction, so that we can learn how to follow God and discover answers to the problems of daily living, and thus show the world a new approach to life.

My Father and my God, how can I thank You enough for giving to me in the Bible the principles I need to live effectively for You in my daily life? Help me to soak my mind in Scripture. In Jesus' name. Amen.

FOR READING & MEDITATION – 2 TIMOTHY 2:14–26

'Do your best to present yourself to God as one approved, a workman who... correctly handles the word of truth.' (v15)

A lecturer in a Christian college received a letter from a former student thanking him for the devotional talks he gave before his morning lectures. The student wrote: 'When I look back to my days at the college I see that those devotionals kept my faith alive.' The lecturer seemed upset by this letter and said to his students: 'How is it possible for a student to be in danger of losing his faith at a Christian college? Why did he depend on eating from my hands? Why didn't he gather food with his own hands?'

I can understand this lecturer's reaction, for I have received many similar letters from people saying, 'I just could not get through the day without *Every Day with Jesus*,' or, 'The thought of *Every Day with Jesus* not being there for me leaves me feeling cold.' A part of me is flattered by such tributes, of course, but always remember that these devotional notes are an aperitif – you should never treat them as the main course. If *Every Day with Jesus* provides your only spiritual input, then you will end up being spiritually malnourished. Explore the Bible for yourself and, if you have access to them, use other resources to help you understand difficult verses.

FURTHER STUDY

Exod. 16:11–36;
Job 23:12;
Jer. 15:16;
Ezek. 3:1–3;
Heb. 5:11–14

1. Why is manna like God's Word?

2. How do we eat God's Word?

All the food you need is in the Scriptures. It's a huge banquet. Don't be a picky eater. Don't nibble – devour. The more knowledge you gain directly from God's Word, the stronger you will be spiritually. My words in *Every Day with Jesus* are soon exhausted, but you will never exhaust the words of Scripture. The Bible gives revelation that is fixed and yet unfolding. So add to goodness spiritual understanding – that is, the knowledge of God, which His book so wonderfully unfolds.

Father, forgive me if I spend a great deal of time in everyday pursuits but little time with You and Your Word. Help me, starting today, to resolve to spend more time in Your Word. In Jesus' name. Amen.

Doing what He likes

FOR READING & MEDITATION – GALATIANS 5:16–26

'But the fruit of the Spirit is love, joy... gentleness and self-control.'
(vv22–23)

To knowledge, says the apostle Peter, we are to add 'self-control'. Or, as *The Message* translates this phrase, 'alert discipline'. The Greek word translated 'self-control' is *enkrateia*, which could be rendered 'take a grip on yourself'. Many in the ancient world regarded self-control as the most important of all the character qualities. The ancient Greeks, for example, spoke much about self-control and claimed that this is where virtue begins. Aristotle (a leading Greek philosopher) said, 'No man is free if his passion fights against his reason and prevails; he is free only when his reason fights against his passion and prevails.'

FURTHER STUDY

1 Tim. 3:1–12;
2 Tim. 2:22–3:5;
Titus 1:5–9

1. Why is self-control essential in leaders?

2. What does a lack of self-control lead to?

The essential difference between self-control as practised by Christians and that practised by non-Christians is that, in the case of unbelievers, they are the centre and thus they control themselves. A Christian who seeks to gain self-control through Christ makes Christ the centre – the spring of action is Christ, not the self. The apostle Paul said in 2 Corinthians 5:14, 'I am controlled by the love of Christ' (Moffatt). The spring of action in Paul's life was love for a Person, the Person of Jesus – in other words, someone other than himself. He was released from self-preoccupation through Christ-preoccupation.

The emphasis of the New Testament is on self-control or alert discipline through love for Christ. St Augustine said, 'Love Christ and do what you like.' When you love Christ, then His likes become Your likes. Every time you are tempted to do something that He does not like, then you will do what He likes rather than following your own dispositions. That is Christian self-control.

Father, I realise that without You I can so easily be mastered by all manner of things. But with You and through You I can be master of everything. This humbles me, yet excites me. I am so grateful. Amen.

Not a cause – Christ

FOR READING & MEDITATION – PHILIPPIANS 4:10–20

'I can do everything through him who gives me strength.' (v13)

I once came across the following statement: 'There is only one way to be an ethical individual and that is to choose your cause and serve it.' The writer, Professor Royce, in an article entitled 'Loyalty', was making the point that central loyalty to a cause makes other loyalties subordinate. 'When you have a cause to give yourself to,' he went on to say, 'then life as a whole is co-ordinated. You don't have to wonder which is first – the cause comes first and you come second.'

How much better, though, when the central loyalty is not some cause, but Jesus. When we give ourselves to Christ we find ourselves in a cause – the kingdom – but the cause is always subordinate to the person. That is why you never hear Christians stand up and say in a testimony service, 'I gave myself to the cause of the kingdom and I found peace and joy.' Rather, they say, 'I gave myself to Jesus and I have found in following Him a joy that I never thought was possible.'

I once counselled a man who had spent countless hours in a rehabilitation centre trying to break free from alcoholism. I wasn't sure if I could help him. However, after explaining that in Jesus we can find a power that gives us the strength to overcome difficulties that defeat us, he got on his knees and gave his life to Jesus, and surrendered all to Him. Immediately, he became a new man and stopped drinking. When I conducted this man's funeral 20 years later, his wife told me he had not touched a drop of alcohol from the day he came to the Lord. She said, 'When he fell in love with Jesus then the lesser loves – his love for alcohol for one – dropped away.' He found self-control through the control of Christ.

FURTHER STUDY

1 Cor. 1:10–25;
Gal. 4:17–19;
6:14–18

1. What was Paul's cause?

2. How did this affect his life?

Dear Father, I see that with You in control of my life I am able to do things I could never do in my own strength. Our relationship means that nothing is impossible, since Your power is linked to mine. Lead on, Lord. I am following. Amen.

The divine exchange

FOR READING & MEDITATION – 2 CORINTHIANS 12:1–10

'But he said to me, "My grace is sufficient for you, for my power is made perfect in weakness."' (v9)

Yesterday, as we talked about the man delivered from alcoholism, the question may have arisen in your mind: Why is it that not all who surrender to Jesus are freed from addictions in the same way? I have met many alcoholics converted to Christ who have struggled for years with their addiction, and maybe you know of some too. Why is it that some are so wonderfully delivered from addictions when they give their lives to Jesus and others are not? Does God have favourites, as He seems to deliver some instantly, yet seems to leave others to struggle?

FURTHER STUDY

Isa. 53:1–12;
1 Cor. 1:26–30;
2 Cor. 5:17–21;
Gal. 2:19–20

1. What was the divine exchange?

2. How is it obtained?

There is no easy answer to this, but it has something to do, I believe, with how desperate the person is at the time when they come to faith. The man I referred to yesterday had reached the point of total despair when I met him, realising that his willpower was inadequate to deal with the problem and that he needed an infusion of power. That infusion of strength came as he surrendered to Christ. From experience, I believe that there are degrees of surrender when it comes to receiving Christ. Some abandon themselves to Him entirely, and their conversion can be dramatic. Others are more tentative. This does not mean that Jesus has not come into their life, but there may still be some inner barriers to be dismantled.

Theologians talk about the 'divine exchange', by which they mean that our sins are put to Christ's account and Christ's righteousness is put to our account. But there is another exchange that takes place within us by the gracious work of His Spirit. The more we surrender to Christ, I believe, the more of Himself He is able to give to us. Totally life-changing.

Father, help me to look to You to find the strength to be really strong. Please save me from so-called strengths that leave me weak. I long to receive Your real strength. Strengthen me and empower me. In Jesus' name. Amen.

Controlled by righteousness

FOR READING & MEDITATION – ROMANS 6:15–23

'When you were slaves to sin, you were free from the control of righteousness.' (v20)

We are reflecting on the truth that from a Christian perspective, self-control is really Christ-control. The more we give ourselves to Him, the more strength we are given to handle those areas of our lives that need to be controlled.

There was a time when I tried to live the Christian life by means of self-control; self-control that was not under Christ's control. At this stage I had just entered my teens and, having been brought up in a Christian home, I realised that my life was not what it should be. So every day I would start out determined to keep myself from sin – not using bad language, not telling lies, developing godly attitudes to those around me and so on. But every night I had to acknowledge my failure. Although I didn't realise it at the time, my problem was that I was trying through self-control to find Christ-control. I had got things the wrong way round, for how could an uncontrolled will control an uncontrolled self. When I was 16, I surrendered my life to Jesus Christ and I began to love Him in such a way that, to use the words of the wife of the alcoholic man we mentioned a couple of days ago, 'all lesser loves dropped away'. I found that when I allowed Christ's love to fill my soul I wanted to do the things that He loved. What my attempts at self-mastery failed to achieve, Christ accomplished in one fell swoop.

Self-control becomes far easier when love for Christ energises us. The will does not function in a vacuum. The will is tied to our emotions – we always do the thing that pleases us. Those who are more concerned about pleasing Christ than pleasing themselves will have no problems with self-control.

FURTHER STUDY

Rom. 6:1–14; 7:4–6; 8:1–17

1. How does sin control us?

2. How does righteousness control us?

Father, I see that the will does not work in a vacuum. Self-control is not simply a matter of willpower – our emotions play a part in it too. Fill me so much with Your love that I will want to please You. Always. In Jesus' name. Amen.

'Holy habits'

FOR READING & MEDITATION – ACTS 24:1–27

'As Paul discoursed on righteousness, self-control and the judgment to come, Felix was afraid... ' (v25)

How interesting that when the apostle Paul stood before Felix and talked about righteousness, the judgment to come, and self-control, the governor was gripped with fear and said, 'That's enough for now!' Many people become nervous when they realise that their attempts to control their life and bring them in line with what is right are proving ineffective.

A word I have not mentioned until now is the word 'discipline'. Once when I was in the United States I was told that a number of pastors have stopped using this word

FURTHER STUDY

1 Cor. 9:24–27;
2 Tim. 4:7–8;
Heb. 12:1–13

1. Why and how does God discipline us?

2. How do we discipline ourselves?

as it causes negative reactions in people's minds. Better to use the phrase 'holy habits', I was told. It's strange that Christians seem to be put off by the word 'discipline', when those involved in sports are not. An Olympic gold medallist said in a television interview, 'It's impossible to reach Olympic standards without strict discipline.' Well, let's be clear about it: to develop and grow spiritually requires discipline and effort. Speak of 'holy habits' if you prefer, but what it comes down to in the end is applying yourself in an alert disciplined way to doing what is right. In truth, there is no freedom without discipline.

A newspaper report, which I have referred to previously, tells how a group of young girls in a private school presented a petition to the Head along these lines: 'We want more freedom, less homework, more TV time, and permission to stay up later at night.' Obviously they wanted to be free from tiresome rules but they had the wrong concept of freedom. I have heard it said that freedom is not the right to do what you want but the power to do what you ought. There is no freedom without self-control.

Father, by Your Holy Spirit, enable me to identify every part of my life where discipline is required and bring these areas under control. I accept that without discipline I cannot be a true disciple. Amen.

Heed the helm or...

FOR READING & MEDITATION – 1 THESSALONIANS 5:1–11

'So then, let us not be like others, who are asleep, but let us be alert and self-controlled.' (v6)

Yesterday we ended with the thought that there is no freedom without self-control. People who try to gain freedom through indiscipline are free in the sense that a boat is free when it loses its rudder; it is free to sail anywhere, even onto the rocks. The rule of the sea applies to life also: heed the helm or heed the rocks.

Elton Trueblood, an American writer and a Christian said: 'The undisciplined person may sit at the piano but he is not free to strike the notes he ought to strike. He is not free because he has not paid the necessary price for that particular freedom.' Many famous individuals have also spoken about the importance of discipline. Edmund Hillary, for example, hailed as the first man to conquer Everest, was asked by an interviewer about his passion for climbing mountains. He replied: 'It's not the mountain we conquer but ourselves.' Peter the Great of Russia is quoted as saying: 'I have been able to conquer an empire but I have not been able to conquer myself.' Hugo Grotius, the Dutch jurist and scholar, said: 'A man cannot govern a nation if he cannot govern a city, he cannot govern a city if he cannot govern a family, he cannot govern a family if he cannot govern himself, and he cannot govern himself unless his passions are subject to reason.'

FURTHER STUDY

Prov. 24:30–34;
1 Tim. 1:18–20;
Heb. 6:7–12

1. Why might some shipwreck their faith?

2. How do we come to experience God's blessings?

In the *Oxford Dictionary of Quotations*, I found that a great many people have highlighted the need for discipline, but none of the quotes, I believe, compares to these words taken from the book of Proverbs: 'Like a city whose walls are broken down is a man who lacks self-control' (Prov. 25:28). There has never been and never will be a great life without self-control.

Father, I long to have done with all mediocrity. May I not be like a city whose walls are broken down. Instead may my life be great – great in You and great for You. In Jesus' name. Amen.

Pause long enough

FOR READING & MEDITATION – JAMES 3:1–13

*'but no man can tame the tongue. It is a restless evil,
full of deadly poison.' (v8)*

The passage before us now shows that an important indicator of whether or not we have self-control is the tongue. The tongue, according to Scripture, is the most ill-disciplined member of our body. Someone has observed that three stages are involved in the act of verbal communication: impulse, consideration, and speech. Unfortunately, many leave out the second stage and jump from impulse to speech. The person who makes every effort to add self-control to their faith pauses between impulse and speech and gives himself or herself to consideration. Your degree of self-control will govern the length of time you pause at the stage of consideration. If you pause too long then it can give the impression of indecision. We should simply pause long enough to be sure that the thing we say is the thing we want and ought to say.

FURTHER STUDY

Prov. 13:3; 15:2;
18:13; 21:23;
Eccl. 5:2–3;
James 1:19–21

1. What does Proverbs teach about consideration?

2. Why does a loose tongue indicate a loose heart?

I was once talking to a pastor and we were only a few minutes into our conversation when he jumped from impulse to speech, bypassing the stage of consideration. He started speaking about some of his congregation in a way that was not appropriate, and in those moments he let me see his emotional immaturity. So disturbing was the manner of his speech that I understood why he was having problems with his other church leaders.

One woman who was growing rapidly in her Christian life admitted: 'The hardest struggle I have ever had is over the word "consideration". I've lived so long on the spur of the moment that I have difficulty in not jumping from impulse to word or act.' The length and strength of our consideration determines our maturity. No consideration, no character.

Father, I see that my tongue can have poison or it can have power. I decide which. Help me to put You at the centre in this aspect of my life. In Jesus' name. Amen.

A double hand-hold

FOR READING & MEDITATION – 1 CORINTHIANS 9:24–27

*'Therefore I do not run like a man running aimlessly; I do not fight
like a man beating the air.' (v26)*

We look now at the quality which, the apostle tells us, must be added to self-control – perseverance. There is little hope of us climbing further up this ladder of characteristics which Peter sets before us unless we understand and practise perseverance. To persevere is to keep on going when everything seems against you. *The Message* paraphrases today's verse in which Paul is talking about perseverance in this way: 'I don't know about you, but I'm running hard for the finish line. I'm giving it everything I've got. No sloppy living for me! I'm staying alert and in top condition. I'm not going to get caught napping, telling everyone else all about it and then missing out myself.' Paul regarded himself as being in a spiritual marathon and would not allow anything to divert him from his goal.

In the 1980 Boston marathon the first female runner to cross the finishing line was a woman by the name of Rosie Ruiz. Amidst cheering crowds and a blaze of lights, she received the winner's medal. But someone noticed that her legs and general demeanour were far too fresh to have run a 26-mile race. An investigation was made, and it was discovered that she had entered the race at the last mile.

How many Christians are like Rosie Ruiz; they want to get in on the finish, but don't want to run the full race! They appear in church on Sundays, but they do not persevere and develop a personal relationship with Jesus through the days of the week. Jesus has told us that a true follower listens to His voice and obeys Him, even if they go through tough times. But He also promises we are held by a double hand-hold that will never let us go (see John 10:27–30).

FURTHER STUDY

Mark 4:1–20;
Rom. 5:1–5

1. Write a definition of perseverance.

2. What causes people to reject the faith?

Heavenly Father, I know You want to use me, and I recognise that I cannot be used unless I am trustworthy. Help me to keep on right to the end with unwavering perseverance. Amen.

Responding to hard times

FOR READING & MEDITATION – 1 CORINTHIANS 16:5–18

'a great door for effective work has opened to me, and there are many who oppose me.' (v9)

Yesterday we referred to the 1980 Boston marathon won by a woman who was later found to have entered the race in the last mile, and duly disqualified. Contrast that runner with those who begin a marathon and finish last. Often they are cheered as much as those who come first. And why? Because everyone recognises the quality of perseverance.

Moffatt translates today's text in this way: 'I have wide opportunities here... and there are many to thwart me.' Many of us may have said, 'I am quitting... I have wide opportunities here but there are too many things against me.'

FURTHER STUDY

2 Cor. 1:3–11;
4:1–18

1. Why did Paul not loose heart?

2. How did he keep going?

One commentator says of perseverance: 'We are summoned to persevere in the truth we have received, to cling to it as a secure handhold in the storm, and to stand firm on this.' Far too many Christians begin well but don't persevere; they don't cling to the truth as a secure hand-hold in the storm, and their lives are strewn with the wreckage of good beginnings but poor endings. We have to face the fact that a number of people do abandon the Christian faith and go back to their old ways (see Matt. 13:1–9, 18–23). In a very early issue of *Every Day with Jesus*, I gave a number of reasons for what was called 'backsliding', and one of the main reasons was that those who did not continue in the faith simply lacked perseverance. They gave up when the going got tough or confusing.

The Christian life is a life full of joy, but we are not immune to life's difficulties. The way in which we respond to these difficulties reveals the degree of perseverance that is in us. As the great preacher C.H. Spurgeon remarked, 'It was by perseverance, after all, that the snail reached the ark.'

God my Father, thank You that although I face difficulties in life, You have said in Your Word that no one can snatch Your child out of Your hand. Help me to never stop walking with You, never to give up. Amen.

Helping others
through life's difficulties

Do you feel called to help others through Christian counselling? Why not explore further training and higher education opportunities at Waverley Abbey College...

If you provide care and support to others or are interested in a career as a counsellor, we provide training to suit a variety of vocational and professional needs. At the heart of all our training is the belief that we are all unique individuals, fearfully and wonderfully made in the image of God, and that every person is intrinsically valuable.

From vocational courses to postgraduate qualifications to continuing professional development, Waverley Abbey College offers a variety of learning opportunities. To find out more or to book your place on a free Open Day, visit **www.waverleyabbeycollege.ac.uk**

WAVERLEY ABBEY
COLLEGE

Growing and learning

FOR READING & MEDITATION – 1 TIMOTHY 4:1–16

'Watch your life and doctrine closely. Persevere in them' (v16)

As we said yesterday, though there is joy in serving Jesus, there are times when the going gets tough and confusing. An unwillingness to face this truth is dangerous. There are some Christians who insist: 'We should never admit to the going being tough and must maintain a positive outlook on everything.' That is why whenever you meet them and ask, 'How are you today?' they respond, 'Wonderful… everything is fine.' Well, there is nothing wrong with having a positive outlook on life (it's better than being negative), but let's also be real. It is not being negative to face the reality that sometimes life is difficult. To deny reality is to diminish yourself and become less of a person, and the unreality will lessen your ability to stand up to difficulties in the future.

FURTHER STUDY

2 Cor. 11:16–33; Acts 26:9–29

1. What were Paul's experiences of life?

2. Why did he persevere?

I once asked a man how things were going in his life. He paused for a moment and said: 'Do you want the usual Christian clichés, or do you want an honest reply?' I told him, 'I want an honest reply.' He responded, 'Well, I am growing and I am learning.' That's the Christian life in a nutshell, isn't it? Sometimes there are more growing and learning days than great and fantastic days.

If the Christian life is anything, it is about persevering in the face of the obstacles and the struggles of life. God gives us the grace to do that, but once again we must throw our will on the side of that grace. 'Triumph,' someone once said, 'is just "umph" added to "try".' There is the need for trusting and there is the need for trying. Keep on trusting and keep on trying. As we do both, we grow.

Heavenly Father, how thankful I am that You are the one who adds the 'umph' to my 'try'. By committing myself to Your Son and His Kingdom I have inherited His strength to persevere. In Jesus' name. Amen.

Life – a task

FOR READING & MEDITATION – HEBREWS 10:19–39

'You need to persevere so that when you have done the will of God, you will receive what he has promised.' (v36)

Victor Frankl, the Viennese psychiatrist, is well known for his persevering through the Nazi Holocaust. The only reason he was not murdered along with his fellow Jews was that he had medical knowledge and was appointed personal physician to several of the Nazi officers. What he endured is beyond description, but he persevered and lived.

After being freed from a concentration camp at the end of the Second World War he wrote: 'The reason so many people are unhappy and seeking help to cope with life is that they fail to understand what human existence is all about. Until we recognise that life is not just something to be enjoyed, but rather is a task that each of us is assigned, we'll never find meaning in our lives and we'll never truly be happy.' Victor Frankl's reasoning makes sense to me, though it may not fit in with what you have been taught since you became a Christian. There are some days, to be honest, when life is really tough and we do indeed do well just to survive. At these times, perseverance is essential.

Another Jew said this: 'We also rejoice in our sufferings, because we know that suffering produces perseverance' (Rom. 5:3). Suffering in this world is here to stay. But, like the apostle Paul, we can rejoice in our sufferings because we know that ultimately the rewards are greater than the cost. When Christian leaders fail, or when the bottom of our world drops out and brutal blows attempt to pound us into the corner of doubt and unbelief, with God's help we can persevere. Without it we stumble and fall. You may have failed before, you may have fallen before, but know right now that by God's grace you can persevere right to the end.

FURTHER STUDY

Acts 13:49–52;
14:8–20;
20:22–24

1. How did Paul consider his life?

2. Do you see life as a task, trial or treasure?

Father, I need to remind myself day by day that if I remain in You then I need never stumble or fall. Heighten my determination to persevere so that I shall be a continual surprise, even to myself. Amen.

Everything can contribute

FOR READING & MEDITATION – PHILIPPIANS 2:12–30

'But even if I am being poured out like a drink offering... you too should be glad and rejoice with me.' (vv17–18)

Yesterday we touched on the difficult subject of suffering, concluding that wisdom dictates we accept that suffering in this world is here to stay. When we acknowledge that fact, then we can start to deal with it.

In *The Screwtape Letters*, which contain the advice of a senior devil to a junior one, C.S. Lewis presents a list of obstacles to perseverance. Among them are matters such as vague guilt, the gradual decay of youthful hopes, old habits, worldly interests, difficulties with the miraculous, doubt, and the demands of God proving inconvenient. It is these matters which the senior devil advises his youthful apprentice to focus on when he sets about tempting humans to sin. These things, claims the senior devil, are points of vulnerability that can be exploited to advantage under the power of temptation. But, says the experienced tempter, it is probably not worth pursuing the matter of suffering. Lewis puts these words in the mouth of the senior devil: 'The Enemy's human partisans have all been plainly told by Him that suffering is an essential part of what He calls "Redemption"... Of course, at the precise moment of terror, bereavement or physical pain you may catch your man when his reason is temporarily suspended. But even then, if he applies to Enemy Headquarters, I have found that the post is nearly always defended.'

FURTHER STUDY

Acts 5:29–42;
16:16–40

1. Why could the apostles rejoice in pain?

2. What was the result?

Once we come to terms with the fact that suffering is a part of life in this fallen world, then we rise above being tempted by it; it loses its hold upon us. There is no suffering that cannot be taken up and used. Acceptance of this fact is probably the greatest safeguard against backsliding. Everything can contribute – even suffering.

Lord Jesus Christ, You who turned Your deepest suffering into a cross of redemption, help me when I am suffering in a lesser way to do the same. Amen.

Using the worst that happens

TUES
7 AUG

FOR READING & MEDITATION – 2 TIMOTHY 1:8–12

'That is why I am suffering as I am. Yet I am not ashamed, because I know whom I have believed' (v12)

William Barclay, in his commentary on 2 Peter, says that the Greek word *hupomone* (which the NIV translates as 'perseverance') means 'the courageous acceptance of everything that life can do to us and the transmuting of even the worst event into another step on the upward way'. When we can take the worst that happens to us and use it to deepen our faith, then perseverance is not a problem for us. We know there is good reason and hope to keep on keeping on. We do not deny that we experience pain, frustration and disappointment – they threaten to overwhelm us. But there is one who can deliver us and be our sufficiency in times of need and help us to use it for His glory (see Psa. 119:153; 2 Cor. 12:9).

This is where the Christian way outshines all other ways. It was said of Jesus by the writer to the Hebrews that 'for the joy set before him [he] endured the cross, scorning its shame' (Heb. 12:2). That is *hupomone* – steadfastness engendered by the knowledge that in the end it will bring joy. It's not a question of looking back but of looking forward. As I have often said before, Christians are like teabags – we are not much good until we have been in hot water. The suffering and troubles that come our way deepen our character and are used by God in His pruning process to make us more like Jesus. I read this in a letter I received which I thought was very appropriate: 'The sufferer is saved by suffering – but only if he or she uses it.'

Hinduism and Buddhism attempt to explain everything that happens, but leave everything as it was before. Christianity explains only what we need to know, but makes everything different.

FURTHER STUDY

Gen. 37:12–36;
50:15–21;
Rom. 8:28–39

1. Why do we not need to fear the worst?

2. How did God use Joseph's troubles for the best?

Father, I am so grateful that Jesus is not just a verbal answer but a vital answer. I can take whatever comes and make it contribute to the rest of my life. Thank You, Father. Amen.

His faithfulness

FOR READING & MEDITATION – MATTHEW 11:1–15

'Blessed is the man who does not fall away on account of me.' (v6)

L ife, it has been said, is determined more by our reactions than our actions. Much of life comes to us without any action on our part – it forces circumstances upon us without our asking or our acting. It is then that reaction counts. You can react in self-pity and frustration, which could lead to a desire to opt out of life, or you can react with courage and confidence that what has happened will improve your character and make you a stronger person.

Malcolm Muggeridge, the famous broadcaster who in later life became a Christian, said that the greatest advances in his life, as far as the growth of his character was concerned, came about not in the happy times but through suffering. When we learn how to persevere and hold on through suffering then something is added to our character that reminds others of Jesus.

FURTHER STUDY

Matt. 24:1–14;
John 6:61–69;
1 Pet. 5:1–9

1. Why are people offended by Jesus and why do they forsake Him?

2. Why did Peter not forsake Jesus?

In concluding these thoughts on perseverance, let me confess that when I was young, this quality was missing in my life. In the 40-something years I have written these notes, which have been published every two months, I have written over five million words. I have been called to persevere, regardless of my natural inclinations. Where does this power to persevere come from? I believe that as I have given myself to Jesus, so He has given Himself to me and enabled me to persevere. Paul said in 1 Corinthians 1:8–9: 'He will keep you strong to the end, so that you will be blameless on the day of our Lord Jesus Christ. God, who has called you into fellowship with his Son Jesus Christ our Lord, is faithful.' His faithfulness has enabled my faithfulness. To this I owe everything. And so, I imagine, do you.

Father, teach me how to rely on Your grace, so that even though many things may discourage me, I will not stop following You or serving You. May I be strong in the strength that comes from You. In Jesus' name. Amen.

Taking God seriously

FOR READING & MEDITATION – PSALM 42:1–11

'As the deer pants for streams of water, so my soul pants for you, O God.' (v1)

We think now about the particular quality that Peter says must be added to perseverance – godliness. The Greek word translated 'godliness' is *eusebeia*, which was used in the pagan world to mean 'piety', 'reverence', 'devotion' or 'religion', so I venture to suggest that the thought here in Peter's mind is that of a deep devotion to God. *The Message* translates this as 'reverent wonder'.

Many years ago, I spoke to a group of young people on the subject of godliness, and before I addressed them I invited them to give me their own ideas on the subject. Here are some of their responses: 'Godliness is living as a recluse... never getting married... dressing down... adopting a simple lifestyle... fasting one day a week... praying for at least an hour a day... not watching television.' While we were still exploring the subject someone asked, 'Can a person be godly and drive a Porsche?' I then explained that godliness – reverent wonder – is an attitude, an attitude towards God Himself. It is not to be confused with outward appearance for, as Scripture puts it, 'The LORD looks at the heart' (1 Sam. 16:7). What is important is that a person is sensitive towards God, following His guidance in everything.

I have chosen the text before us today because I feel it shows us the real meaning of godliness: the godly person has a heart that pants after God. He or she will be, as Tommy Tenney once said, 'a God-chaser'. A godly person can be young or old, rich or poor, of any race, colour, culture or temperament. None of the things I have just mentioned matter; what does matter is the individual's inner desire to chase after God, to walk with Him, and to take Him seriously.

FURTHER STUDY

Psa. 63:1–11; 84:1–12

1. What are the characteristics of a God-chaser?

2. Which characteristics do you have?

God my Father, make me a God-chaser, I pray. Touch my heart in a new and fresh way today so that, like the psalmist, I will thirst for You and pant after You. In Jesus' name I pray. Amen.

To know Him better

FOR READING & MEDITATION – EPHESIANS 1:15–23

'I keep asking that… God… may give you the Spirit of wisdom and revelation, so that you may know him better.' (v17)

Yesterday we said that in the heart of a godly person there is a deep desire to pursue God. Examine the life of a godly person and two things will emerge: a longing for God and a willingness to follow Him in all matters. Dr W.E. Sangster defined godliness as 'absorbing attention and utter obedience'. In other words, godliness or reverent wonder is giving God our undivided attention and complete obedience.

Take first the thought of giving God our full attention. This is manifested by attending to God in prayer. On my bookshelf are several biographies of the great saints of the past – men such as Augustine and John Wesley, and women such as Teresa of Avila and Catherine Booth – and their biographers unite in confirming the importance they all attached to the time they gave to prayer. One interesting thing about their praying is that few of their prayers were for themselves. It seems the closer one gets to God in prayer, the less one prays for oneself.

FURTHER STUDY

Exod. 33:15–34:8;
Matt. 6:5–15;
James 4:1–3

1. What was Moses' desire?

2. How should we pray?

Sadly, the prayers of some people are entirely for themselves. Some years ago, this prayer was found among the papers of a British Member of Parliament who lived in the eighteenth century: 'O Lord, Thou knowest I have mine estates in the City of London and likewise that I have lately purchased an estate in the county of Essex. I beseech Thee to preserve the two counties of Middlesex and Essex from fire and earthquake, and as I have a mortgage in Hertfordshire, I beg Thee likewise to have an eye of compassion on that county. For the rest of the counties Thou mayest deal with them as Thou art pleased.' Outwardly, prayer may be a holy occupation but we can so easily get off track when it is all focused on ourselves.

Gracious and loving heavenly Father, in teaching me more about the power of prayer, please save me from all selfishness I pray. I long to know You for Yourself, not for what I can receive from You. Amen.

Reflecting perfection

FOR READING & MEDITATION – 2 CORINTHIANS 3:7–18

'And we, who... reflect the Lord's glory, are being transformed into his likeness with ever-increasing glory' (v18)

Those whose hearts are set on pursuing God are careful not to misunderstand and misuse prayer in the manner of the British MP whose prayer request we looked at yesterday. In fact, personal petition almost disappears from their prayer times, though not entirely, of course. Intercession for others keeps its place, but thanksgiving, praise and worship comprise most of their praying. It is in this reverent wonder of God that we find the first steps to godliness. The godly look at God, and He looks at them, and their godliness flows from this contemplation of God and enjoyment of His presence.

Perhaps no verse puts it more clearly than the text before us today, in which the apostle Paul speaks of 'reflecting as in a mirror the glory of the Lord' (Amplified). That is how godliness is gained. As I have said in previous issues of *Every Day with Jesus*, a Christian who gazes on the Lord and remains still and steady before Him becomes a mirror in which the likeness of Jesus is seen more and more clearly. Yet more than a reflection is seen. A transformation takes place, as if the mirror is changed by the reflection that falls on it. It was said of Francis of Assisi that he was the 'mirror of perfection'. The godly, allowing for the idiosyncrasies of personality in all of God's people, reflect perfection.

Understand this: the more time we spend with God in prayer, the more we become like Him. If we don't spend time in prayer, we almost make Him irrelevant to our lives. To pursue godliness, then, is to spend time with Him, to attend to Him, to enjoy Him and to become caught up in reverent wonder.

FURTHER STUDY

Psa. 34:1–22;
Luke 2:36–38;
Acts 6:8–15

1. What happens to those who look to God?

2. How did Anna serve God?

Father, forgive me that so much of the time I am absorbed by things that divert my attention away from You. Help me to gaze on You until I become a mirror in which the likeness of Jesus is seen more and more clearly. Amen.

The morning's first thought

FOR READING & MEDITATION – PSALM 143:1–12

*'Let the morning bring me word of your unfailing love,
for I have put my trust in you.' (v8)*

We continue reflecting on the thought that godliness is, in Sangster's words, 'absorbing attention and utter obedience'. Many years ago I talked to an elderly Christian, who was a devout and godly man, about the definition of godliness we are reflecting upon at the moment. I asked him if he agreed with this. When he said that he did, I asked him what approaches he used in his own life which helped him to become absorbed in giving God his attention.

This was his response: 'There are many things, but two things in particular help me keep my focus on Him, the first being this: every morning when I awake, I immediately think about the Lord. Before I speak to anyone else I speak to Him. I offer no more than a sentence or two, such as, "Thank You, Lord, for the joy of spending another day with You," or, "All glory be to You, Father, and to Your Son and to the Holy Spirit." My real prayer time follows later, but I find that opening myself up to God in the first moments of the day sends the message to my soul that God is my first and most important focus.'

FURTHER STUDY

Psa. 5:1–7;
57:7–11;
Lam. 3:21–26;
Mark 1:35

1. What is fresh every morning?

2. How did Jesus start the day?

It is significant, I think, that other godly people have the same practice. John Stott said that when he woke in the morning he swung his legs over the bed and said, 'Good morning heavenly Father, good morning Lord Jesus, good morning Holy Spirit.' There is something about tilting your spirit in the direction of God as soon as you begin your day that is spiritually powerful. My pastor during my youth – a very godly man – used to say, 'The first thing I do when I awake, before I even wash my face, is to wash my thinking in the thought of Christ.' I commend this practice to you. Try it and see what happens.

Father, grant that my first thought of the day and my last thought at night shall be of You. May I be more absorbed with You than with any other person or thing. In Jesus' name. Amen.

Praying through Scripture

MON
13 AUG

FOR READING & MEDITATION – PSALM 23:1–6
'The LORD is my shepherd, I shall lack nothing.' (v1)

We talked yesterday about the practice of many godly people of focusing their first thoughts of the day on God. Another powerful practice I have discovered in godly people is that of praying through Scripture. To pray through Scripture means taking a passage and using it to talk to the Lord in prayer.

Take Psalm 23 as an example. One could pray something like this: 'Father, I thank You that You are my shepherd. Because of this I shall not want for any good thing. I am so grateful, too, that You make me lie down in green pastures and lead me beside quiet waters. The way You restore my soul in times when I am assailed by troubles, and the way You guide me in the paths of righteousness, showing me the difference between right and wrong, is something for which I can never thank You enough. Death was my enemy, dear Lord, before I knew You, but now I am not afraid of that dark shadow, for I sense Your protecting hand over my life. I know I will die but I know, too, that I will live again. What a comfort that is to me. How I bless You, also, for Your anointing that covers me from the crown of my head to the tip of my toe. Because You delight in me and continually pour into my life Your endless love, my cup always runs over. You do not leave me with a half-full experience; Your generosity causes me to overflow. Blessed be Your name forever.'

Just reading God's Word turns our attention to God, of course, but praying in this way sharpens our focus even more. When a godly person taught me to pray like this – through Scripture – my prayer time was transformed and God became more real to me. I recommend this practice to you also.

FURTHER STUDY

Psa. 100:1–5;
121:1–8;
Acts 4:23–31

1. How did the apostles pray and what was the result?

2. Pray through Psalm 100 and Psalm 121 yourself.

God, You breathed into words and they became Your Word. Help me to saturate my thoughts with Your thoughts so that I cannot tell where my mind ends and Yours begins. In Jesus' name. Amen.

'To will one will'

FOR READING & MEDITATION – 1 PETER 4:1–11

'he does not live the rest of his earthly life for evil human desires, but rather for the will of God.' (v2)

We move on now to a second aspect of the definition of godliness or reverent wonder we have been looking at over the past few days – 'obedience'. Not only do the godly give their attention to God, they also follow and obey Him. And not in a resigned manner, but in trust, and deep respect and faith, even in the face of confusion.

One consequence of reverent wonder is that it results in longing to 'will one will' with God, and to know Him even more. And, when we are walking with Him so closely, the need to coax and cajole our wills so that they are in harmony with the will of God is no longer a struggle. We can say, as Jesus did to His Father, 'I have come to do your will, O God' (Heb. 10:7). And for Jesus, doing God's will was not simply a duty; it was a delight. The godly are invariably in a state of glad obedience. They are not overly concerned when they do not know the reasons for God's will; they follow just the same.

FURTHER STUDY

Psa. 40:6–8;
Heb. 10:1–24

1. Why did Christ delight to do God's will?

2. What was the result?

Many Christians want to know 'Why?' The godly only want to know 'What?' – 'What would You have me do in this situation?' Job chapters 38–41 are a wonderful poetic description of how creation is subject to God's will from the farthest constellations, to the waves of the sea, to an eagle soaring at His command. Likewise, in the Psalms, hills, rivers, sea, mountains and trees all rejoice at the coming of the Lord to judge the earth (Psa. 96; 98) and worship songs and hymns down to the present day declare creation's glad obedience to God's will. If the creation itself joins in the chorus of heaven saying, 'Thy will be done,' then how much more can we bow the knee and say with Saul of Tarsus, 'Lord what do you want me to do?' (Acts 9:6, NKJV).

Father, how I long to reach this place where I obey Your will for my life, not only utterly but instantly and gladly. May Your will always be my delight, not only today but for ever. Amen.

Good in Your sight

FOR READING & MEDITATION – MATTHEW 11:25–30

'Yes, Father, for this was your good pleasure.' (v26)

We are seeing that the godly are not overly concerned when they do not understand the reasons for God's will. They follow in faith just the same. In the eighteenth century, at the time of The Enlightenment (or The Age of Reason), Christians were criticised for regarding human reason, even at its best, as being an unreliable guide. Reason always wants to know 'Why?' The godly, however, are more interested in knowing *what* they should be doing than in knowing why God allowed a difficult situation to arise. A friend of mine says that whenever a misfortune occurs in his life, his instinctive reaction is to wonder how he can co-operate with God so that the worst can be turned into the best.

The idea that we have to consider the merit of any direction that God gives before it is obeyed is weighed by the growing disciple. They may use their reason in times of confusion and crisis to ensure they are clear what God's will is but, once they know it, in faith and trust they follow the guidance they have been given. In trusting God, we recognise that here on earth we will may never fully understand the purposes of God with our finite minds. Tragedy may come, but by faith we learn to see it only as a blessing in disguise and would say with William Cowper:

> *Behind a frowning providence*
> *He hides a smiling face.*

We can learn that all things are in loving hands and that when difficulties and distress occur, in faith and trust we ask God to bring good out of it. In every event the godly say, 'Even so, Father, for it seemed good in Your sight' (Matt. 11:26, NKJV).

FURTHER STUDY

Gen. 22:1–19;
Psa. 146:1–10;
Heb. 11:17–19

1. Why was Abraham prepared to sacrifice Isaac?

2. Why should we not put total trust in human leaders?

Father, I realise I am made in the very structure of my being for Your will. You are my life and my way of life. May I walk in Your will every day of my life. In Jesus' name. Amen.

Hold fast!

FOR READING & MEDITATION – JOHN 15:18–27

'If they persecuted me, they will persecute you also.' (v20)

The great hymn writer Charles Wesley wrote this line in one of his hymns: 'Mould as Thou wilt Thy passive clay.' There is a passive and an active side to obedience. Passive obedience involves a willingness to be moulded by the hands of the divine Potter. But obedience is active also in the sense that we put into action the instruction and guidance and revelation given to us by God – even when it might lead to personal discomfort, imprisonment or the loss of life. This might sound harsh and challenging but God gives grace and strength for times of need.

FURTHER STUDY

Matt. 5:10–12;
John 16:1–4;
2 Tim. 3:12;
James 1:12

1. Why might we suffer persecution?

2. Why might this be a blessing?

A few years ago, a man in a country where Christians were being persecuted wrote to me and said, 'I know that some day I might have to give my life in the cause of Christ.' Some time later, his parents, who were aware that he had written to me, contacted me and gave me this news: 'Our son was killed by some religious fanatics who shot him as he was coming out of church.' As *Every Day with Jesus* is read in many countries of the world, it is possible that I am talking to someone right now whose loyalty to Christ is about to result in them being fiercely persecuted. Hold fast to Christ, my dear friend. The prayers of the family of God are with you this very hour.

What God has done through the ready obedience of His children down the running ages is amazing. It is true that 'everyone who wants to live a godly life in Christ Jesus will be persecuted' (1 Tim. 3:12), but at the same time the world takes note of those whose lives are God-centred. Godliness is the Christian on his knees in reverent wonder and the Christian on his feet in complete obedience. It is as simple and as profound as that.

Father, we cry out to You today to be with every one of Your children who is undergoing persecution. Help them to be faithful to You in all things. Help me, too, to be a faithful disciple – on my knees attentive, on my feet obedient. Amen.

'Christians are not angels'

FOR READING & MEDITATION – ROMANS 12:9–21

'Be devoted to one another in brotherly love. Honour one another above yourselves.' (v10)

To godliness, says the apostle Peter, we are to add brotherly kindness (2 Pet. 1:7). To grow in the Christian life we not only pursue God, but we also pursue good relationships with everyone. Godliness that focuses only on God and does not flow out into our relationships with others is not true godliness.

If we find personal relationships a nuisance, then there is something amiss. Brotherly kindness flows out from reverent wonder of God. However, at the same time it is something we 'make every effort' to cultivate, because even Christians are not angels! Once, after I had made that comment, a man remarked, 'Many of my acquaintances are angels.' 'What do you mean?' I asked, somewhat surprised. He explained, 'They fly up in the air over the slightest thing!'

It has been said that 'to be is to be in relationship'. In other words, we do not come to a full awareness of who we are until we are in a relationship with another. Those who have suffered bad relationships in their developmental years may have difficulty in being sure of their own identity. Leslie B. Salter, an American writer, says: 'Every normal man or woman longs more keenly for warm friendship, admiration and human responsiveness from his or her circle of friends and acquaintances than for anything else in life.' Start giving others what they long for. There is nothing wrong with that. Start today by developing, as *The Message* translates today's verse, 'warm friendliness' and kindness to those around you. Don't wait until tomorrow – start today. The kindness that you show is likely to come back to you in dozens of different ways. But even if it doesn't, you will be the better for the giving.

FURTHER STUDY

Col. 3:12–17;
1 Thess. 4:9–10;
Heb. 13:1–3;
1 Pet. 1:22

1. What is brotherly kindness?

2. How does it operate?

Heavenly Father, forgive us that sometimes we try to make our brothers and sisters a means to our own benefit. Save us from manipulating others and help us give just for the sake of giving. In Jesus' name. Amen.

Life works just one way

'Love your neighbour as yourself.' (v31)

We continue reflecting on the importance of good relationships. Unless our relationships proceed along the line of certain inherent laws, they break down. We are advised in today's text to 'love your neighbour as yourself'. That is a law of life, the way God has ordained relationships to function.

Of course, you may decide not to love your neighbour as you love yourself, but if that happens you are no longer free; you are caught up in another law – the law of degeneration. When we don't love our neighbour as ourselves, then we won't get along with ourselves. You see, you don't resolve any problems with your neighbour by not loving them, you simply make a problem for yourself. We cannot make or bypass these laws of relationships – we only discover them. They are written into life by a pen other than our own. People may try with great skill to make life operate in their way but it will not work.

FURTHER STUDY

John 13:34–35;
Eph. 5:1–2;
1 John 3:11–19

1. Why are we to love others?

2. How are we to love others?

It has been said that there are five ways in which people relate to others. (1) Some try to dominate others. (2) Some stay aloof from others. (3) Some are indifferent to others. (4) Some work with others. (5) Some work with and for others. Which of these ways of relating are closest to God's original design?

Take the first: suppose you try to dominate others – what happens? Relationships snarl up and then break down. A newly married young man is said to have remarked, 'In the home I tried to be "it" but I found my wife to be "oppos-it".' Dictators try to follow this way and rise only to fall. The nature of reality is against them. They may stay in power for a while but eventually they will fall. As Jesus said, 'all who draw the sword will die by the sword' (Matt. 26:52).

Father, may I not dominate others or control them but come alongside them and reflect the way in which You relate to me. In Jesus' name. Amen.

A recluse – off balance

FOR READING & MEDITATION – 1 THESSALONIANS 4:1–12

'Now about brotherly love... you yourselves have been taught by God to love each other.' (v9)

Yesterday we said that there are five ways in which people relate to each other. The first, we noted, is the attempt to dominate others – a relational style that is ultimately controlling and abusive. The second way is to stay aloof from them. This is the opposite swing of the pendulum; if we cannot dominate others then we will stay aloof from them. But can we avoid human relationships and retreat into our shell without this affecting us? No, we cannot.

Sometimes shyness is really a desire not to be rejected. Usually it is an attitude that is fuelled by fear – fear of other people. Some, however, may stay away from others because they feel inferior to them and think they are not worthy to be in a relationship with them. There are those, too, who stay away from others because they feel superior to them and look down on them.

FURTHER STUDY

Luke 16:19–31; 18:9–14

1. How was the rich man a recluse?

2. How was the Pharisee a recluse?

We are made inherently for relationships and any attempt to live apart from others brings dis-ease to our personalities. You break the law of relationships just as much by withdrawing from others as you do by trying to dominate them. One person cannot be isolated without distress. That is why to be withdrawn is to be off balance – he or she is trying to live against the laws of the kingdom. Those who have entered the kingdom of God are called to 'warm friendliness' and mutual affection.

If withdrawing from people will not work, then neither will the third method of relating – being indifferent to others. You cannot remain indifferent to others and remain untouched. Your attitude will result in frustration. Indifference is reckless and risky. You may find that others are indifferent to you. You will meet yourself coming back.

Father, I see that I cannot escape relationships, for they are built into the very fabric of Your universe. Help me, in the love that You give me through the Holy Spirit, to be kind and friendly to everyone with whom I am connected. Amen.

Grace – for the taking

FOR READING & MEDITATION – PHILIPPIANS 2:1–11

*'Each of you should look not only to your own interests,
but also to the interests of others.' (v4)*

Another way in which we can relate to others, as we have already noted, is to work with them. This sounds as if it has an edge on the other ways of relating, but it can also be inadequate. It is possible to work with others and yet withdraw our life from them. When I say this, I am thinking particularly about relationships in the Church. So sensitive are these laws of the kingdom that if we hold back from others, our relationships will break down.

There is only one real way of relating that God has ordained – we work not only with others but also *for* others. To have the other person's best interests in mind as well as your own – a desire to help the other person as you yourself would like to be helped. If this really was practised in our churches, then a solution would be found for almost every problem. In John 13:34–35, we find the most life-changing truth as spoken by Jesus: 'A new command I give you: Love one another. As I have loved you, so you must love one another. All men will know that you are my disciples if you love one another.'

FURTHER STUDY

Luke 9:1–6;
John 12:1–8;
1 Cor. 10:23–
11:1;
Eph. 6:5–9

1. How did Judas work with others yet withdraw his life?

2. How should relationships work?

Just imagine the impact it would have in the world if we could really embrace this – it would revolutionise all our relationships at church, our families, individuals, our work colleagues and even between nations, where an atmosphere of mutual mistrust previously existed. What would the world look like if we genuinely thought more about the needs of others and loved as Jesus loves us?

There is no doubt that this is challenging, but we have been granted access to God's grace and heaven's resources. Let's show willing, and let God multiply.

Father, give me this attitude of mind that looks not only to my interests but also to the interests of others. Your grace is there to enable me to do this; help me to draw on it. In Jesus' name. Amen.

Just passing by!

FOR READING & MEDITATION – LUKE 10:25–37

*'A priest happened to be going down the same road, and when he
saw the man, he passed by on the other side.' (v31)*

I have always thought that our text for today is one of the
saddest verses in the whole of Scripture. The priest in
Jesus' story seemed to pass by with complete indifference
and watched the man who had been assaulted by robbers go
through agony. He did not seem to care.

That same attitude – the attitude of not caring – seems to
be increasingly common in our contemporary society. I once
heard a journalist comment, 'We have many crises in our
world but one of the greatest is the crisis caused by the lack of
care.' So how do we live out our lives in a world where
there is little care for one another? We keep on caring.
To allow other people and their attitudes to determine
our own responses and behaviours is not God's way.

Shakespeare, as you probably know, wrote some
words that are in harmony with Scripture: 'Love is
not love which alters when it alteration finds' (Sonnet
116). Brotherly kindness – true brotherly kindness,
that is – does not change no matter what changes
there are in others. It was said of John the Baptist
that he was 'a voice… calling in the desert' (Matt. 3:3).
Someone has remarked that the difference between
a voice and an echo is that a voice is proactive and an echo is
reactive. Are we echoes or are we voices?

Years ago, a missionary doctor contracted typhus while
caring for patients. Yet when he heard that a woman would die
if she did not have a Caesarean operation, he told his colleagues
to carry him to the operating room, and operated on her as he
was dying. Perhaps the woman never knew about this, and
maybe she did not care. But he cared – and that is enough.

FURTHER STUDY

Ezek. 16:4–14;
Luke 15:1–7;
Gal. 6:1–3;
James 2:8

1. Why do we pass others by?

2. Why should we seek to help others?

**God, help me to bring to all my relationships an attitude of care
and concern that will help lighten other people's loads. Save me
from just passing by. In Jesus' name. Amen.**

Kindness lives on

FOR READING & MEDITATION – EPHESIANS 4:17–32

*'Be kind and compassionate to one another, forgiving each other,
just as in Christ God forgave you.' (v32)*

Today's text is one I repeat to myself almost every day. It has within it all the music of the grace of God. Look at the words that precede it. What a contrast. They call our attention to matters that are dismal and depressing: bitterness, rage, anger, brawling, slander, malice. It is as if the clouds have rolled across the sky blotting out the sun, as so often happens on a grey winter's day in Britain. Then suddenly we come across the words, 'Be kind and compassionate to one another, forgiving each other,' and it seems as we read that instruction that the sun has come out once more, bringing warmth, colour and comfort to the soul.

FURTHER STUDY

Matt. 15:29–39;
26:6–13;
Acts 9:36–42

1. How did Jesus and Dorcas model kindness?

2. Why does kindness live on?

Two things in particular about kindness are, I think, worth noting. One is that no one ever regrets being kind. There are many things I have done during my life that I regret, but I have never regretted being kind. The other thing to note about kindness is that an act of kindness lives on in the memory when other things have long been forgotten. Luke, writing a long time after the shipwreck off Malta, remembered the kindness of the inhabitants and said, 'The islanders showed us unusual kindness' (Acts 28:2). A poet who obviously did not understand Christianity wrote:

*So many gods, so many creeds,
So many paths that wind and wind.
When all that this sad world needs
Is just the art of being kind.*

Kindness is not 'all that this sad world needs', but it is something it needs. May we help to meet its needs through some act of kindness we do today.

Father, help me to do some act of kindness this day that will live on in someone's memory for ever. May I cover all acts of unkindness with the same robe of kindliness with which You have covered me. Amen.

Ten Words

When Moses descended from Mount Sinai with two stone tablets, he brought with him so much more than a set of instructions. He'd had a face-to-face encounter with the living God, who had outlined for the newly emancipated Israel 'ten words' – to be foundational laws for life.

Join us as we explore each of the Ten Commandments and how they are still so crucial to our spiritual freedom today.

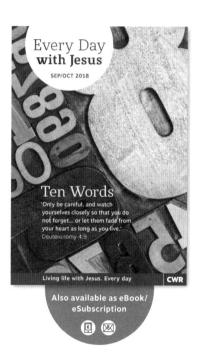

Also available as eBook/ eSubscription

Obtain your copy from CWR, a Christian bookshop or your National Distributor.
If you would like to take out a subscription, see the order form at the back of these notes.

A change of perspective

FOR READING & MEDITATION – 1 CORINTHIANS 10:14–22

'Is not the cup of thanksgiving for which we give thanks a participation in the blood of Christ?' (v16)

Jesus' manifesto carries a twofold expectation: first, that we give ourselves unreservedly to Him, and second, that we give ourselves wholeheartedly to each other. A double giving is required of us – to God and to others. I am talking now, of course, about our relationships with one another as brothers and sisters in Christ. Those who belong to God belong also to everyone else who belongs to God. There is no relationship in the universe as real and as wonderful as the relationship we enjoy with each other through our relationship with Jesus Christ.

FURTHER STUDY

Acts 2:42–47;
4:32–37;
6:1–3

1. How did the Early Church practise *koinonia*?

2. How could you deepen your fellowship with other believers?

The Greek word *koinonia*, translated 'fellowship' or 'communion', though not originally a Christian word, was adopted by the Church and given a new content. In the text before us today, Paul uses that word to describe the participation we have in Christ when we break bread together in His name. *Koinonia* now means much more than it did in pagan times. The word has been redeemed. Relationships in the Church are quite different from those in the world – or can be.

Simon Peter, the very one whose advice we are seeking to follow in this issue, once said to Jesus, 'Supposing they are all disconcerted over you, I will never be disconcerted, never' (Matt. 26:33, Moffatt). These words express a 'they–I' attitude. Peter was superior, aloof, self-righteous and critical. But following repentance, he was filled with the Spirit and we notice the change from 'they–I' to 'we': 'Why do you stare at us?' (Acts 3:12); 'If we are being called to account today… ' (Acts 4:9); 'For we cannot help speaking' (Acts 4:20). He had changed his perspective. And how!

My Father and my God, help me understand the relationship You have brought me into since I came to know You and became part of Your Church. Help me connect with others – truly connect. In Jesus' name. Amen.

Loved everlastingly

FOR READING & MEDITATION – JEREMIAH 31:1–9

'I have loved you with an everlasting love; I have drawn you with loving-kindness.' (v3)

We come now to the last quality on Peter's list – love (2 Pet. 1:7). It is no surprise that the ladder of Christian virtues should end in love. Warm friendliness is wonderful, but the love that Peter says we should 'make every effort to add to [our] faith' is a reflection of that *agape* love that God has shown to us.

How different is God's love from the natural love that we find in our hearts! The love we offer others is often conditional love – the kind that says: 'Love me and I will love you;' 'Do this and you can count on my love.' This love is not like the love of God. We are not loved by God for what we do, and no failure can rob us of His love. While sin can cause a break in the relationship, it does not stop God loving us.

This love is initiated in heaven: 'We love because he first loved us' (1 John 4:19). That is the great thing about *agape* love – it initiates. This is, in part, why we cannot 'explain' why God loves us. To explain it would require Him to love us for some reason but, as we have seen, He loves us for ourselves alone. He chose to love because He *is* love. Nothing in us gave rise to His love and nothing in us can extinguish it. It is love without condition and it is love without end.

Read today's text again: 'I have loved you with an everlasting love.' When we think about this kind of love, the poverty of our own love comes over us and we realise our love is not like the love of God. How amazing to know we are loved everlastingly. The apostle Paul rejoiced in this truth when he cried, 'Who shall separate us from the love of Christ?' (Rom. 8:35). Divine love is love without reason and without end.

FURTHER STUDY

Deut. 7:7–9;
Psa. 103:1–22;
John 3:16

1. What causes God to love us?

2. What causes us to love God?

Father, with all my heart I ask, help me make love my aim. Strengthen my love as I grow in Your likeness. I cannot be less than love and live – really live, that is. Amen.

The chemistry of love

FOR READING & MEDITATION – GALATIANS 5:16–26

'But the fruit of the Spirit is love, joy, peace, patience, kindness, goodness, faithfulness' (v22)

No human being can love as fully as God loves, but we can love with our whole being. To live, as we said yesterday – to really live – is to love. Every fruit of the Spirit is related to love. Love is at the head of the list and underlies all the rest. The miracles that God works in us, He works by the chemistry of love. Nothing else will free us of the destructive self-centredness that resides within us and is the root of all sin – putting ourselves in the place God has reserved for Himself.

Passion is a very powerful force in our lives and through it we can achieve many things. However, passion is most powerful when it is wedded to *agape* love. Passion alone can blind us to the imperfections of a loved one; love (*agape* love) sees the imperfections and loves just the same. Passion can be hungry, demanding love; divine love is generous, eager to be shared, releasing. Passion can suddenly turn to anger and destroy the object of its affections, but love is never ungovernable and is always creative.

FURTHER STUDY

2 Sam. 13:1–29;
John 15:12–13

1. Contrast passion and love.

2. Why does passion fail but love never fail?

The sole route to freedom is the way of love. Nothing but pure love deposited in us and received from God's love can release our imprisoned natures and bring us to maturity. As we become generous in loving, we become free. 'Salvation,' said Daniel Rowlands, a great Welsh preacher of a past generation, 'is really learning from our Lord how to love.' 'You ask me for a method of obtaining perfection,' said St Thérèse of Lisieux, 'I know of love and love only.' The most significant spiritual growth is growth in love. Without love all other growth is cancerous, it is consuming instead of constructing. If love is lacking, everything is lacking.

Father, when I think of the ways in which You love me and have reached out to me and changed me, my prayer is that my love might reach out to others and change them also. Grant that this may be so. In Jesus' name. Amen.

You are loved

FOR READING & MEDITATION – GALATIANS 2:11–21

'The life I live in the body, I live by faith in the Son of God, who loved me and gave himself for me.' (v20)

How does this love of which we are speaking – divine love – come to us? This is where many go wrong. They think they can stir it up or manufacture it by an act of will. A woman once told me, 'I simply must try to love the Lord more'. She thought that love was merely a matter of willpower. Divine love does not spring up inside us; it comes down into us from God.

Once when I was in Nairobi a man approached me and said: 'I have read your writing for years and I notice that there is one message, one central emphasis, that you come back to time and time again. The first time I read it, it didn't make much impact on me, but the second and third times it hit with all the force of a hurricane.' I thought I knew what he meant but I wanted to make sure, so I asked, 'What is that one central message?' He replied, 'It is that you can truly love only when you know you are loved.' He was right. I constantly repeat this message because I meet so many Christians who think that loving God is a matter of effort. The practical outworking of that love may take effort, but the love that fills us comes not by frantic effort but by fully realising how much we are loved. Love, the love that comes from God, is our response to His love. His *agape* creates *agape* in us.

Heaven knows no higher strategy for depositing love in human hearts than to bring us to the cross and hold us there. As we see how much we are loved and as the scales fall from our eyes, our own love is set on fire in response to God's love. This, I believe, was what Paul was thinking about when he wrote today's verse. It was the centre of Paul's rich devotional life. Let it be your centre too.

FURTHER STUDY

Psa. 136:1–26;
Eph. 3:14–19

1. Why and how does God repeat His message of love?

2. What was the central emphasis of Paul's prayer?

Father, I see that this is the crux of everything. I love because I am loved. And what a love! Your love has taken hold of me. Let it grow in me more and more. Amen.

'A village God'

FOR READING & MEDITATION – 1 TIMOTHY 2:1–15

'I urge, then, first of all, that requests, prayers, intercession and thanksgiving be made for everyone.' (v1)

The love that springs up within us once we know we are truly loved by God does not remain parochial, it begins to embrace the wider world. Christians receive with reverent wonder that God loves us personally, but we also know that He does not love us exclusively. 'God so loved the world', says that most beautiful text in the Bible, 'that he gave his one and only Son' (John 3:16). This amazing love moves out to all whom God has created. Every man and woman in the universe is the object of His ceaseless and generous love. When divine love flows into us from God above, how can we help but love as He loves? How can we fail to see everyone with the vision God intends us to have?

FURTHER STUDY

Matt. 28:18–20;
John 3:14–17;
Acts 11:27–30;
17:22–34

1. How can we have a global vision?

2. What are our global responsibilities?

John Stott told of slipping into a village church on holiday once, and feeling rather uncomfortable as he listened to the prayer offered by the person who was leading the service. The prayer lasted only for a minute or two and focused solely on the needs of the congregation and the village. Since there were no prayers for the wider world, John Stott concluded that this was a village church with a village God! Love from God enlarges our perspective so that it takes in not just our immediate community but the whole world.

Look again at the passage before us today, in which is highlighted that 'prayers, intercession and thanksgiving [should] be made for everyone – for kings and all those in authority'. As we focus on the truth that we are loved by God, a transformation takes place and we find we cannot deny that love to anyone. We discover, too, that we love not with our own love but with a given love, given by the Holy Spirit, which moves us to embrace all humankind.

Father, give me this love – love for everybody – and may it infuse all my actions. All I have to do is to surrender to Your love. Help me to do that more and more. Amen.

Love that is unconditional

FOR READING & MEDITATION – 1 JOHN 4:7–21

'Dear friends, since God so loved us, we also ought to love one another.' (v11)

Yesterday we reflected on how a vision of God's love for us widens our own vision so that it takes in the whole world. Many times I have sat in counselling sessions with Christian workers who, as we shared together, came to realise that the service they thought they had given out of pure love for God was, in fact, tainted by self-love. It was conditional love. A missionary once told me: 'I loved people in order to convert them. My attitude to them was this: share my faith, believe in the God I believe in, follow Him and serve Him the way I serve Him, and I will continue to love you.' Even a mother's love – what someone has called 'the nearest to heavenly love of all the loves of earth' – can become smother love if the child's freedom to be himself or herself is stifled by the mother's self-interest. God's love is not like that: He loves us without imposing conditions and without bargaining with us. Those who follow Jesus learn to love people with an unconditional love. We do not love people in order that they will stop getting drunk, or that they will attend church, or even that they will love God in return for our love. We can learn to love them for themselves alone and go on loving them even when they reject the gospel, question the motives that drive us, and accuse us of having self-serving purposes.

In all our relationships, we follow the pattern of loving that God has shown to us, namely to love unconditionally. This path is not an easy one. It led Jesus to the cross, and over the centuries it has led many to lay down their lives as a martyr. But there can be no compromise. It is love and love only. It is love without reason that saves.

FURTHER STUDY

Luke 23:8–46; Rom. 5:6–8

1. How did Jesus model unconditional love?

2. Contrast man's love and God's love.

Father, by Your grace and with Your help I intend my love to be as prodigal and indiscriminate as Your love. Let there be no blocking of that love in me this day or any day. In Jesus' name. Amen.

FOR READING & MEDITATION – 1 JOHN 5:1–5

'This is how we know that we love the children of God: by loving God and carrying out his commands.' (v2)

We spend another day reflecting on the thought that the love flowing through us to others is to be unconditional. Yesterday we said that even the love of a mother – that most powerful of loves – is not always exempt from self-centredness. It can be possessive at times, and resentful of other loves. Sadly, many parents have interfered in a child's relationship with others, simply because they could not bear the idea of their child loving someone else more than themselves.

Then think also of those who we sometimes refer to as 'do-gooders'. On the surface, it might seem noble and unselfish to dedicate one's life to doing good to others, but the underlying motive may be tainted by a desire to bolster a fragile ego. A woman wrote to her vicar because she was being harassed by an over-zealous church visitor. 'Please stop Miss So-and-So saving her soul through me,' she begged. In another church, where a do-gooder went around looking for individuals to whom they could do good, it was said you could tell the victims by their hunted look. There is a difference between doing good and being a do-gooder. The do-gooder does good because of the good feelings he or she gets from doing the good, whereas those who do good act in a kindly manner because they cannot do otherwise. Their warm friendliness and generous love flows from them without condition. This is the pure flame of love, the supernatural love that God pours in the soul of those whose hearts are open to receive it.

FURTHER STUDY

Matt. 6:1–4;
Luke 6:27–36;
Titus 3:8

1. Why may 'doing good' be bad?

2. What motivates people to do good?

Divine love is without taint and without end. It has insight, patience, infinite resources and, though it delights when it is reciprocated, it makes no such demand.

Gracious and loving Father, the more I learn of Your love, the more I long to love as You love. Once again I reach out to You so that Your love might flow into me and rise until my love is as Your love. Amen.

Nothing is real but love

FOR READING & MEDITATION – 1 CORINTHIANS 13:1–13

'Love never fails.' (v8)

We are as mature as our love. That is the thought that has held our attention over the past few days. The more the world explores the nature of things, the more it comes to see the centrality of love. Human love, though tainted with self-centredness, can on occasions rise to great heights. Laplace, a famous French mathematician and astronomer, said when he was dying, 'Science is mere trifling… nothing is real but love.'

An international congress on mental health once declared that the taproot of mental ill health is not caused so much by a chemical imbalance but rather a lack of love. Sociologists often trace recklessness and carelessness to a lack of love. Our prisons are full of men and women who were never loved. Love, even imperfect human love, has wonderful therapeutic value. Anyone who has studied adolescent psychology (a subject close to my heart) knows that love is the soil in which our nature grows. The more one is loved, the more one flourishes. We are the products of those who loved us or did not love us, and who did or did not pour their lives into ours.

FURTHER STUDY

Gal. 5:6;
2 Thess. 3:3–5;
1 Tim. 1:5–17

1. What is the goal of Christian teaching?

2. Where does love come from?

Paul says in the verse before us today that love never fails. Honesty compels us to admit that sometimes it seems to fail. A devoted mother dies while the son is still wayward. A loyal wife continues to love but her husband still has affairs. A faithful pastor continues to feed God's sheep with little or no response. Has love failed in these cases? Love may not instantly win a response, but love itself does not fail. The person who loves and goes on loving finds himself or herself all the better for loving. The world's greatest need is the kind of love that keeps on loving.

Father, You have taught me through Jesus and Your Word the way of love. May I take that way and go no other way. Help me attempt to melt every situation by love, and even if this fails, to go on loving still. In Jesus' name. Amen.

'Whining for a chairlift'

FOR READING & MEDITATION – 2 PETER 1:1–11

'For this very reason, make every effort to add to your faith goodness; and to goodness, knowledge' (v5)

On this our last day together we return to the passage with which we started our meditations on the theme 'Guaranteed'. We have considered that we are to 'make every effort' to add to our faith seven characteristics, like seven rungs of a ladder, and as we do so it will add a depth and richness to our lives. But we are not expected to do this in our own strength, for laying behind it are the power and promises of God (vv3,4).

We saw, too, that each rung is to be negotiated step by step. However all of us experience times in our Christian life when we wish things were easier, when we wish we didn't have to undergo self-discipline. But there is no way to avoid such times. It's best to accept this fact and get on with life.

FURTHER STUDY

Prov. 4:1–27;
Luke 9:23–26;
Phil. 3:1–21

1. Why might we never stumble?

2. Why might we stumble?

Bridger Wilderness Park in Wyoming, USA, like many other places of interest, invites visitors to place their comments in a suggestion box. These are a few of the suggestions made. 'Please avoid trails that go uphill.' 'Chairlifts need to be put in some places so that we can get to wonderful views without having to hike.' 'Escalators would help.' 'A McDonald's would be helpful in places.' Someone commented: 'The wildness of the wild stretches out and towers in all directions but people miss it, whining for a chairlift, pining for a McDonald's, or chafing at the bugs.' Don't miss out on what God has for you because of the challenge to cultivate these characteristics.

To change the metaphor, the Christian life is a journey. That means taking one step after another. Just keep going and let God have His way in you. Add to your faith the qualities we have thought about and, as we said at the beginning, you will never drop out of the march. That's guaranteed!

My Father and my God, thank You for this spiritual journey I'm privileged to take with You. In the knowledge that Your grace is multiplied to me, help me now to add. In Jesus' name. Amen.